Disney Theatrical Productions
under the direction of
Thomas Schumacher
presents

Music and Lyrics by
KRISTEN ANDERSON-LOPEZ and ROBERT LOPEZ

Book by
JENNIFER LEE

Based on the Disney film written by JENNIFER LEE and directed by CHRIS BUCK and JENNIFER LEE

Starring
CAISSIE LEVY PATTI MURIN
JELANI ALLADIN GREG HILDRETH JOHN RIDDLE
ROBERT CREIGHTON KEVIN DEL AGUILA TIMOTHY HUGHES ANDREW PIROZZI
AUDREY BENNETT MATTEA CONFORTI BROOKLYN NELSON AYLA SCHWARTZ
ALYSSA FOX AISHA JACKSON ADAM JEPSEN

ALICIA ALBRIGHT TRACEE BEAZER WENDI BERGAMINI ASHLEY BLANCHET JAMES BROWN III CLAIRE CAMP
LAUREN NICOLE CHAPMAN SPENCER CLARK JEREMY DAVIS KALI GRINDER ASHLEY ELIZABETH HALE ZACH HESS DONALD JONES, JR.
NINA LAFARGA ROSS LEKITES AUSTIN LESCH SYNTHIA LINK TRAVIS PATTON ADAM PERRY JEFF PEW OLIVIA PHILLIP
NOAH J. RICKETTS ANN SANDERS JACOB SMITH NICHOLAS WARD

Co-Producer
ANNE QUART

Technical Supervision
AURORA PRODUCTIONS

Senior Production Supervisor
CLIFFORD SCHWARTZ

Production Stage Manager
LISA DAWN CAVE

General Manager
RANDY MEYER

Associate Director
ADRIAN SARPLE

Associate Choreographers
SARAH O'GLEBY
CHARLIE WILLIAMS

Casting
TELSEY + COMPANY
RACHEL HOFFMAN, CSA

Orchestrations
DAVE METZGER

Executive Music Producer
CHRIS MONTAN

Music Coordinators
MICHAEL KELLER
MICHAEL AARONS

Music Director
BRIAN USIFER

Hair Design
DAVID BRIAN BROWN

Makeup Design
ANNE FORD-COATES

Special Effects Design
JEREMY CHERNICK

Additional Dance Arranger
DAVID CHASE

Sound Design
PETER HYLENSKI

Video Design
FINN ROSS

Puppet Design
MICHAEL CURRY

Scenic and Costume Design
CHRISTOPHER ORAM

Lighting Design
NATASHA KATZ

Music Supervision and Arrangements by
STEPHEN OREMUS

Choreographed by
ROB ASHFORD

Directed by
MICHAEL GRANDAGE

ISBN 978-1-5400-3322-2

DISTRIBUTED BY
HAL•LEONARD®

Visit Hal Leonard Online at
www.halleonard.com

Contact Us:
Hal Leonard
7777 West Bluemound Road
Milwaukee, WI 53213
Email: info@halleonard.com

In Europe contact:
Hal Leonard Europe Limited
Distribution Centre, Newmarket Road
Bury St Edmunds, Suffolk, IP33 3YB
Email: info@halleonardeurope.com

In Australia contact:
Hal Leonard Australia Pty. Ltd.
4 Lentara Court
Cheltenham, Victoria, 3192 Australia
Email: info@halleonard.com.au

Mattea Conforti, Ayla Schwartz

Patti Murin

Jelani Alladin, Andrew Pirozzi

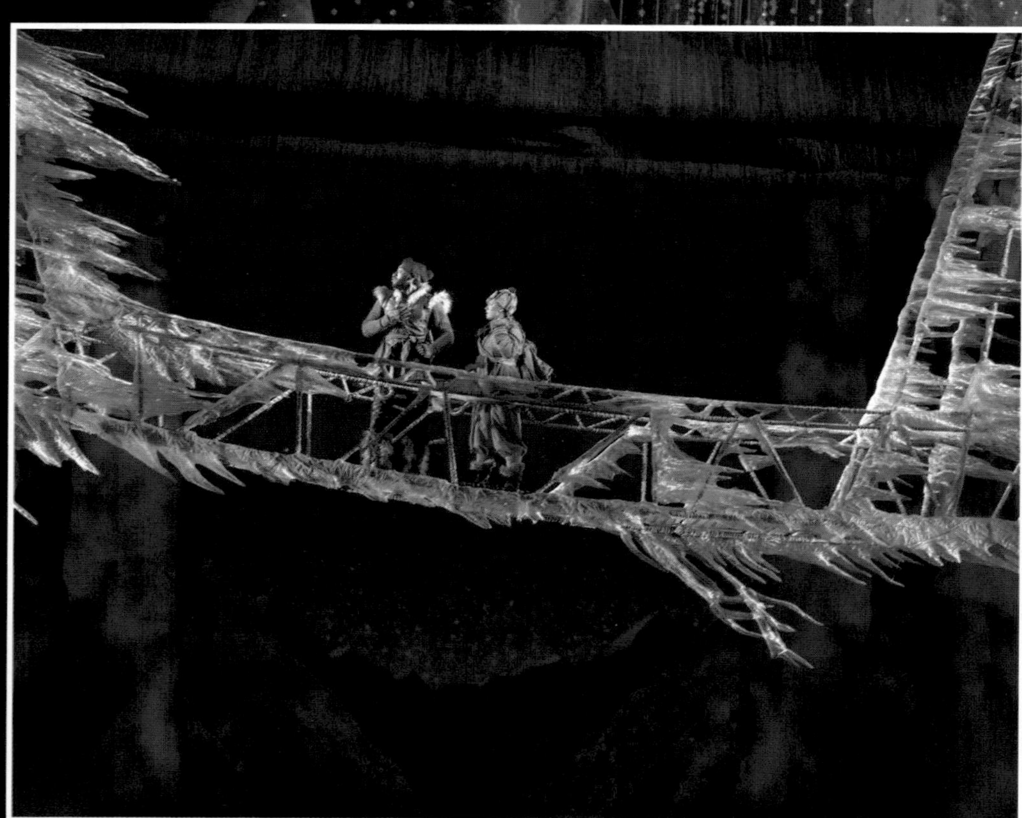

Jelani Alladin, Patti Murin

Caissie Levy

Patti Murin, John Riddle

Synthia Link, Caissie Levy, Patti Murin

A LITTLE BIT OF YOU

Music and Lyrics by KRISTEN ANDERSON-LOPEZ
and ROBERT LOPEZ

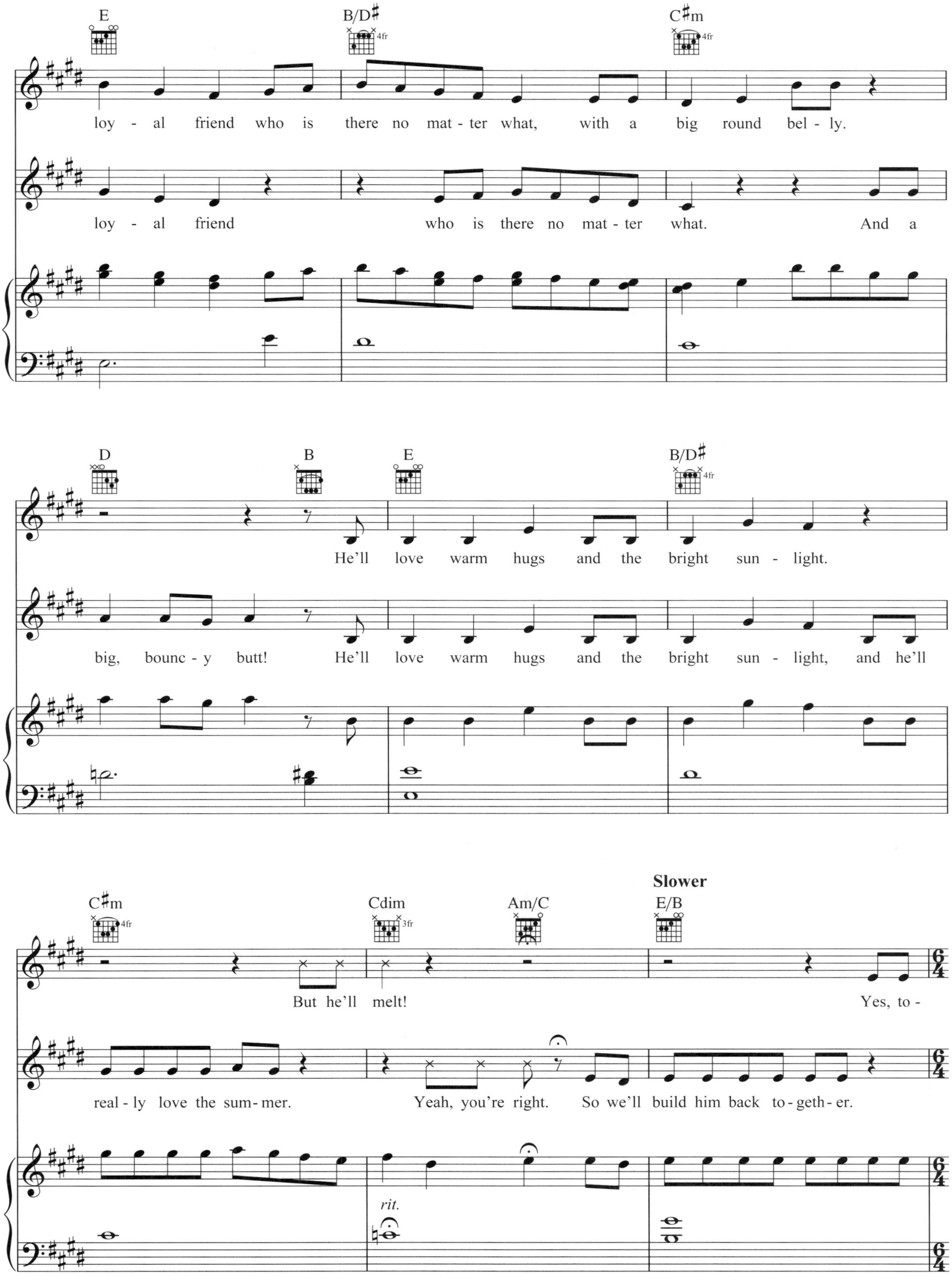
E
B/D♯
4fr
C♯m
4fr
loy - al friend who is there no mat - ter what, with a big round bel - ly.
loy - al friend who is there no mat - ter what. And a
D
B
E
B/D♯
4fr
He'll love warm hugs and the bright sun - light.
big, bounc - y butt! He'll love warm hugs and the bright sun - light, and he'll
Slower
C♯m
4fr
Cdim
3fr
Am/C
E/B
But he'll melt! Yes, to -
real - ly love the sum - mer. Yeah, you're right. So we'll build him back to - geth - er.
rit.

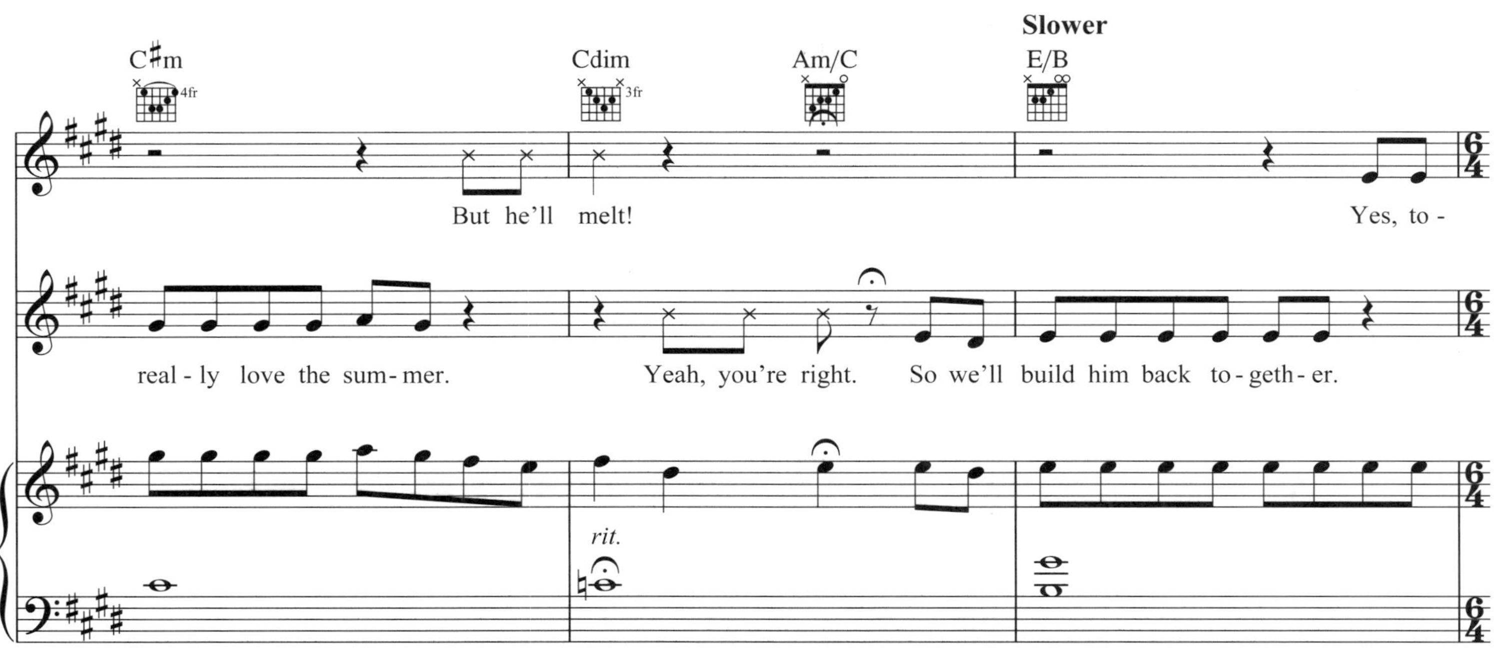

YOUNG ELSA: *Okay. Time for bed.*
YOUNG ANNA: *NO. Time for more magic please and thank you.*
YOUNG ELSA: *Anna, you know I'm not supposed to even be doing this.*

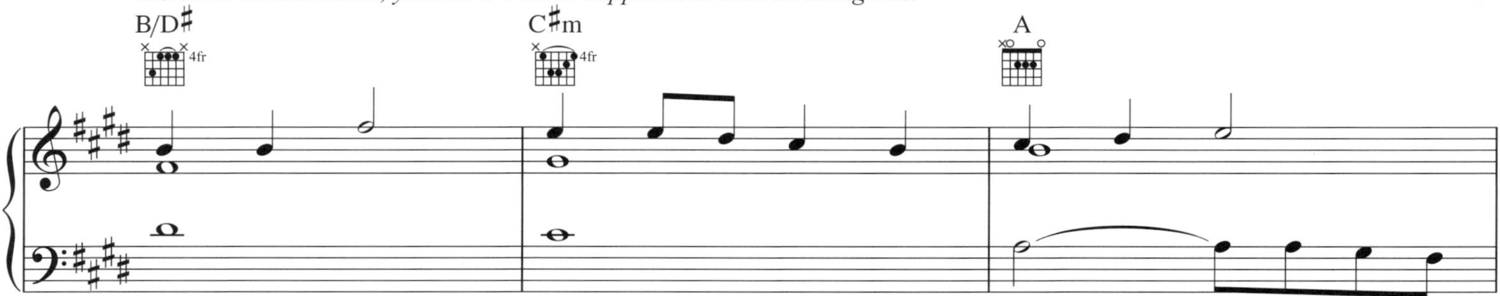

YOUNG ANNA: *But your magic is the most beautiful, wonderful, perfectful thing in the whole wide world.*
YOUNG ELSA: *Do you really think so?*
YOUNG ANNA: *Yes! So, do it, please, before I burst from inside to outside.*
YOUNG ELSA: *Okay. Okay. Don't burst.*

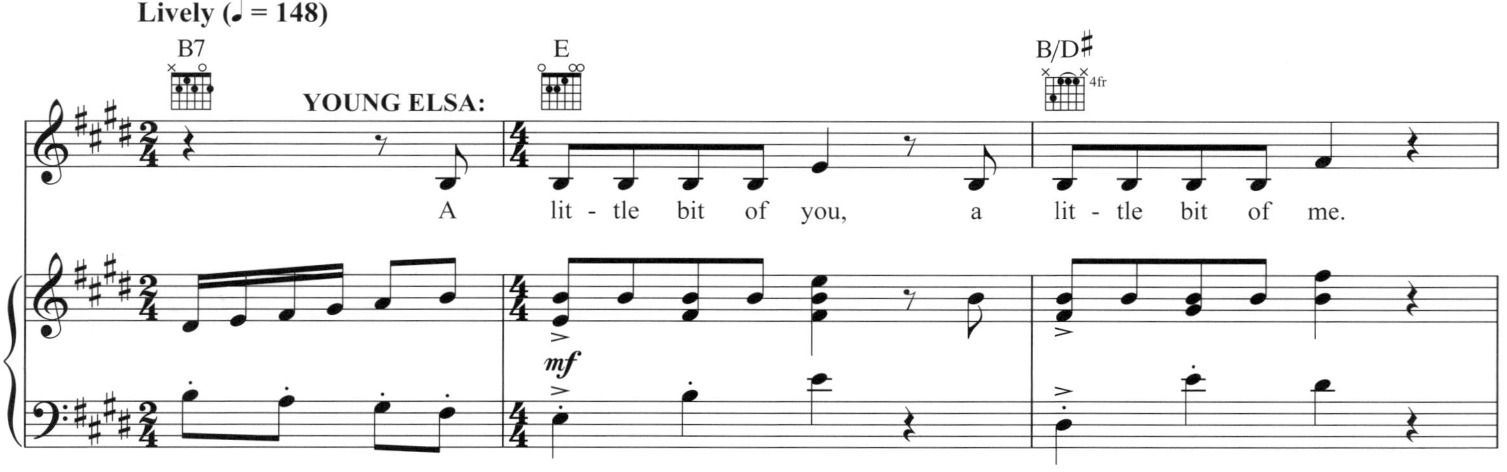

Faster (♩ = 157)
C♯m
4fr
A
E
YOUNG ELSA:
A lit - tle bit of fun.
YOUNG ANNA:
You do the mag - ic and I get to see.
Lit - tle bit of
poco a poco accel.
B/D♯
4fr
C♯m
4fr
A
Cdim
3fr
E
A lit - tle bit of mag - ic and it all takes flight!
fun in the mid - dle of the night.
B/D♯
4fr
C♯m
4fr
G♯m
4fr
D/F♯
B7
La la la la la la la la la la la la la la la la la la la la.
This is so a - maz - ing! More! More! More!

Faster yet (♩ = 176)
A5
D(add2)
Lit-tle bit of you.
Lit-tle bit of
Mag - ic! Mag - ic! Do it, El - sa, do it more!
8va
f
B♭5
F5
Gm7
B♭5/D♭
me.
Me! Me! Me! Me! Me! Me! Lit-tle bit of you, lit-tle bit of me! Yip - pee!
(8va)
ff
Bsus/C
A7♯5
loco
3
3
f

DO YOU WANT TO BUILD A SNOWMAN?
(Broadway Version)

Music and Lyrics by KRISTEN ANDERSON-LOPEZ
and ROBERT LOPEZ

A♭(add2)
Gm7
E♭maj9/G
We used to be best bud - dies and now we're not. I
Dm7♭5
G7
Cm
Cm7
F7
Fm7(add4)
wish you would tell me why. Do you want to build a snow - man?
mp
A♭m/C♭
YOUNG ANNA:
It does - n't have to be a snow - man. YOUNG ELSA: Go away, Anna. O - kay,
E♭(add2)
C♭/G♭
C♭
bye.
(knocking)
cresc.
f

Moderately (♩ = 157)
B♭
E♭(add2)
6fr
Do you want to build a snow - man,
or ride our bike a-round the
mf
sim.
B♭(add2)/D
A♭/C
Cm
3fr
halls?
I think some com - pa - ny is o - ver - due.
I've start - ed
B♭m
E♭
6fr
talk - ing to the pic - tures on the walls.
Hang in there, Joan.
It gets a lit - tle
A♭
4fr
E♭/G
3fr
G
G7/F
lone - ly,
all these emp - ty rooms.
Just watch - ing the hours tick
mf

Tempo I (♩ = 146)
Cm/E♭
3fr
E♭+/F
by.
(tongue clicks)
3
f
C♭
YOUNG ANNA: Elsa?
B♭
mp legato
p
Slower, freely (𝅗𝅥 = ♩)
N.C.
ANNA:
ANNA: Elsa?
Please, I know you're
E♭sus2
6fr
B♭/D
in there. I'm just won-d'ring how you've been. Do you may-be want to

A♭/C
Cm
3fr
Gm
3fr
take a walk, or sit and talk, or let me in? Are you read - y for to -
A♭(add2)
4fr
B♭/D
E♭
6fr
G7sus/D
G7/D
3
mor - row? It's your big day! Is there an - y - thing I can
Gm7/C
F7
ELSA:
do? ___
Do you wan - na build a
E♭/G
3fr
A♭
4fr
B♭
N.C.
E♭(N.C.)
snow - man?

FOR THE FIRST TIME IN FOREVER
(Broadway Version)

Music and Lyrics by KRISTEN ANDERSON-LOPEZ
and ROBERT LOPEZ

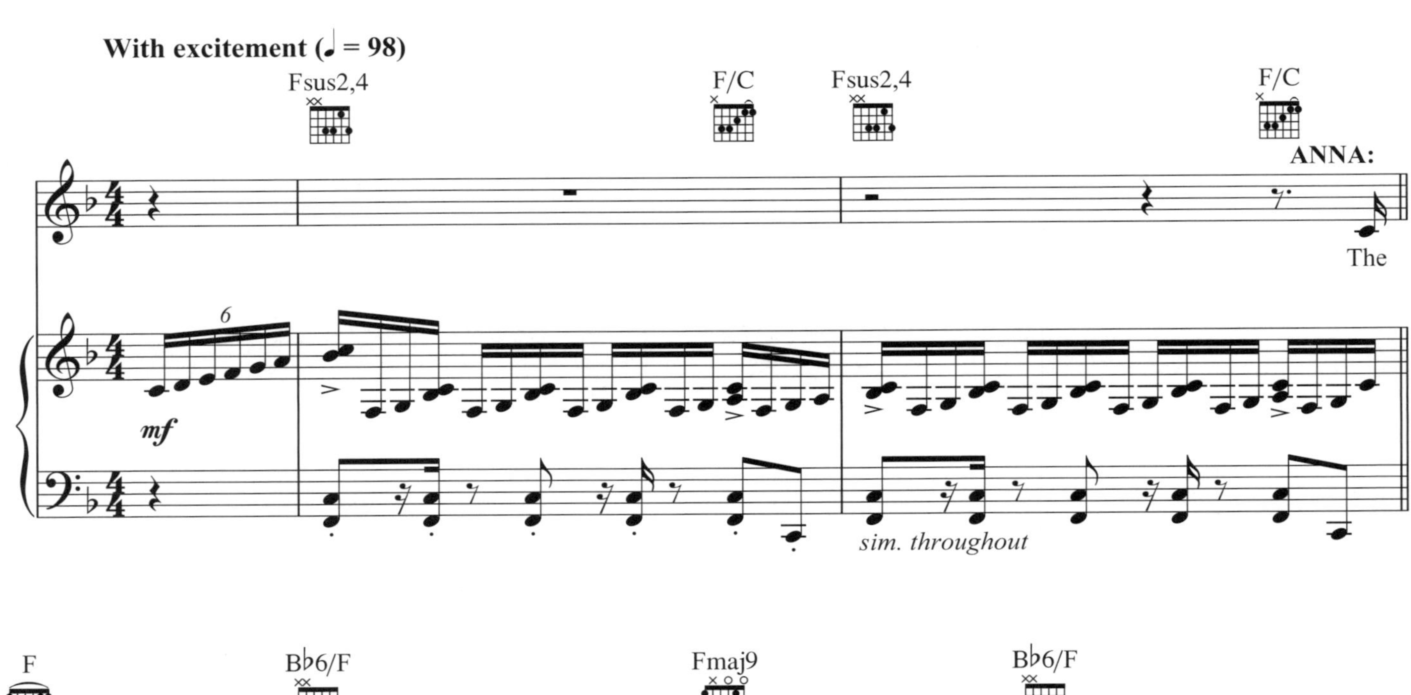

F
B♭6/F
Fmaj9
B♭6/F
years I've roamed these emp - ty halls.
Why have a ball - room with no balls?
Dm
Dm/C
Bm7♭5
G9
9fr
Cor - o - na - tion day is just the best!
There'll be
Em
Fmaj7
Em/G
Am9
5fr
ac - tu'l real live peo - ple.
It' - ll be to - tal - ly strange.
But
E♭(add2)
6fr
C9sus
C
wow! Am I so read - y for this change!
For the

Slightly faster (♩ = 102)
F/A
F/B♭
B♭
C/E
first time in for - ev - er there'll be mu - sic, there'll be light.
f
F(add2)
F/E
C/E
Dm
Am
For the first time in for - ev - er I'll be
E♭
6fr
A7
Dm
Dm/C
danc - ing through the night. Don't know if I'm e - lat - ed or gas - sy, but I'm
B♭6
G9/B
9fr
F5/A♭
3fr
F/B♭
some - where in that zone. 'Cause for the first time in for - ev -

Fsus/B♭
C7sus
- er
I won't be alone.
Tempo I
Fsus2,4
F
Fsus2,4
F
Fsus2,4
F/C
ANNA: I can't wait to meet everyone...What if I meet THE ONE?
To-
mp
mf
G♭
C♭6/G♭
G♭maj9
C♭6/G♭
night, i-mag - ine me, gown and all,
fetch-ing-ly draped a - gainst the wall, the
G♭
G♭(add2)/B♭
D♭sus
D♭
pic-ture of so-phis - ti-cat - ed grace.
I

G♭
C♭6/G♭
G♭maj9
3fr
C♭6/G♭
sud-den-ly see him stand - ing there, a beau-ti-ful stran - ger, tall and fair. I
E♭m
6fr
E♭m/D♭
Cm7♭5
A♭7
4fr
wan-na stuff some choc - 'late in my face! But then we
Fm
G♭maj7
Fm/A♭
B♭m7
laugh and talk all eve - ning, which is to - tal-ly bi - zarre.
E
D♭sus
4fr
D♭
4fr
Noth-ing like the life I've led so far. For the

Slightly faster (♩ = 104)
Gb/Bb
Gb/Cb
Cb
Db/F
Gb(add2)
Gb/F
Db/F
first time in for-ev - er there'll be mag-ic, there'll be fun. For the
Ebm7
Bbm
E
first time in for-ev - er I could be no-ticed by some-one.
Bb7
Ebm
Ebm/Db
Cb6
Ab9/C
And I know it is tot-al-ly cra - zy to dream I'd find ro - mance,
Gb5/A
Gb/Cb
Gbsus/Cb
but for the first time in for-ev - er,

Db7sus
4fr
Gbsus
Db/F
at least I've got a chance!
8va
mp
Eb5
6fr
Bbm
Ab/C
ELSA:
Don't let them in,
don't let them see.
(8va)
Db
4fr
Ab5
4fr
Abm/Cb
4fr
Be the good girl you al-ways have to be.
Eb5
6fr
Bbm
Ab/C
Con - ceal.
Don't feel.
Put

D♭
A♭5
A♭m/C♭
on a show, make one wrong move and ev - 'ry - one will
E♭5
D♭/F
know.
But it's on - ly for to-
G♭
G♭/F♭
A♭/E♭
A♭/G♭
ANNA:
It's on - ly for to - day!
It's ag - o - ny to wait!
ELSA:
day.
It's ag - o - ny to wait.
WOMEN:
Ooh
Ooh
MEN:
Ooh
Ooh
mp cresc.

Am7♭5
F9
The gate!
Tell the guards to o - pen up the gate!
Ah,
Ah,
the gate, the
Ah,
the gate, the
Ah,
the gate, the
rall.
a tempo
cresc.
For the
gate, the gate!
gate, the gate!
ff
6

G/B
Cmaj9
first time in for - ev - er I'm get - ting
Don't let them in, don't let them
D/F♯
G
G(add2)/F♯
what I'm dream - ing of. A
see. Be the good girl you al - ways have to
Em
Bm
F
chance to leave my lone - ly world, a chance to find true love.
be. Con - ceal.

B7
E/G♯
A(add2)
For the first time,
Con - ceal. Don't feel. Don't let them know.
WOMEN:
For the first time in for - ev - er we're no
WESELTON, HANS, & MEN:
For the first time in for - ev - er we're no
B/D♯
E
B/D♯
C♯m7
ANNA:
For the first time in for - ev -
long - er shut out - side.
For the first time in for - ev -
add KRISTOFF:
long - er shut out - side.
For the first time in for - ev -
4fr

G♯m
4fr
D
B7
B7/D♯
-er the gates are o-pen wide. I
-er the gates are o-pen wide.
-er the gates are o-pen wide.
Em
G/D
C
A7/C♯
A
know it all ends to-mor-row, so it has to be to-day! 'Cause for the
cresc.
8va
5
G/B
C(add2)
G/D
A7/E
first time in for-ev-er, for the first time in for-ev-
The first time, the first time
the first time,
The first time, the first time

Cm/E♭ 3fr D7sus C(add2)/D 3fr G(sus2/4) G/D

- er, nothing's in my way!

in for-ev - er.

WOMEN:

To -

in for-ev - er.

KRISTOFF, HANS, WESELTON, & MEN:

To -

mf

G(sus2/4) G/D G(sus2/4) G/D G

day!

day!

6

6

cresc.

HANS OF THE SOUTHERN ISLES

Music and Lyrics by KRISTEN ANDERSON-LOPEZ
and ROBERT LOPEZ

Cm/E♭ G/D G/C F(add2) F(add2)/E D N.C. G/B Am/C
3fr
very small islands to the south. And nobody sings about
D Em Am G/B G/C Dsus
this humble face or my lack of grace or quotes what comes out of my
Più mosso
Gsus G C G/B F G C
3fr
mouth. Thank goodness. I've journeyed a long way to see your sister crowned. To
Faster
Dm Am B♭ F A
honor and to back you, yet here I go and smack you to the ground.
dim.
poco rit.

Quicker, earnestly
Dm
B♭sus2
F(add2)
Am/E
Please ac - cept the hum - blest of a - pol - o - gies from a clum - sy prince who's on - ly come to
mp
poco rit.
D
G
Dm7/G
C
serve and please with a line of mean big broth - ers that goes on for miles! A
molto cresc.
molto rit.
f
Tempo I
G
G/F
G/E
G/E♭
G/D
Csus2
3fr
man you won't see in a stat - ue of bronze, just Hans of the South - ern
Slower
N.C.
G(add2)
G/B
C(add2)
G(add2)
Isles.
mp
rit.

DANGEROUS TO DREAM

Music and Lyrics by KRISTEN ANDERSON-LOPEZ
and ROBERT LOPEZ

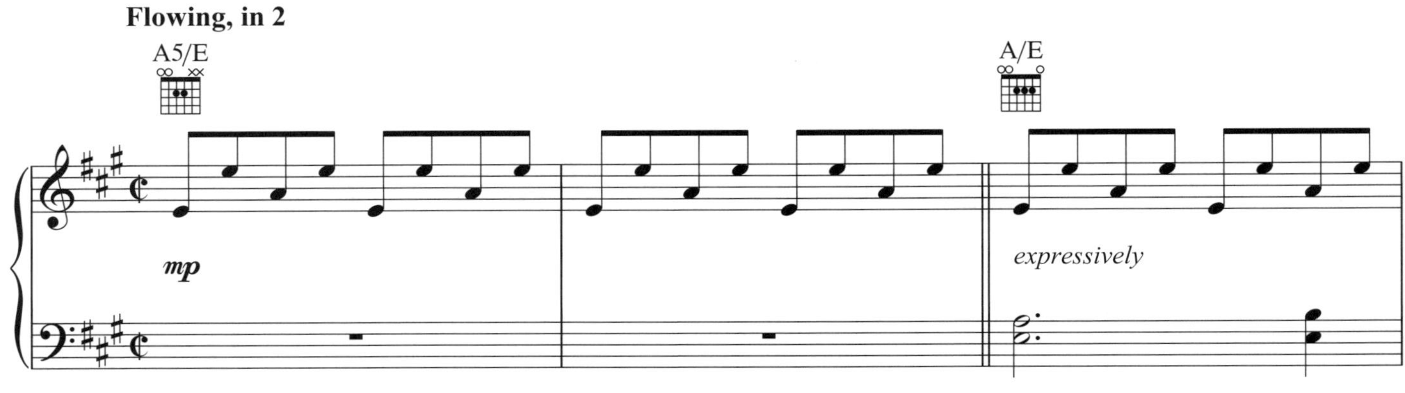

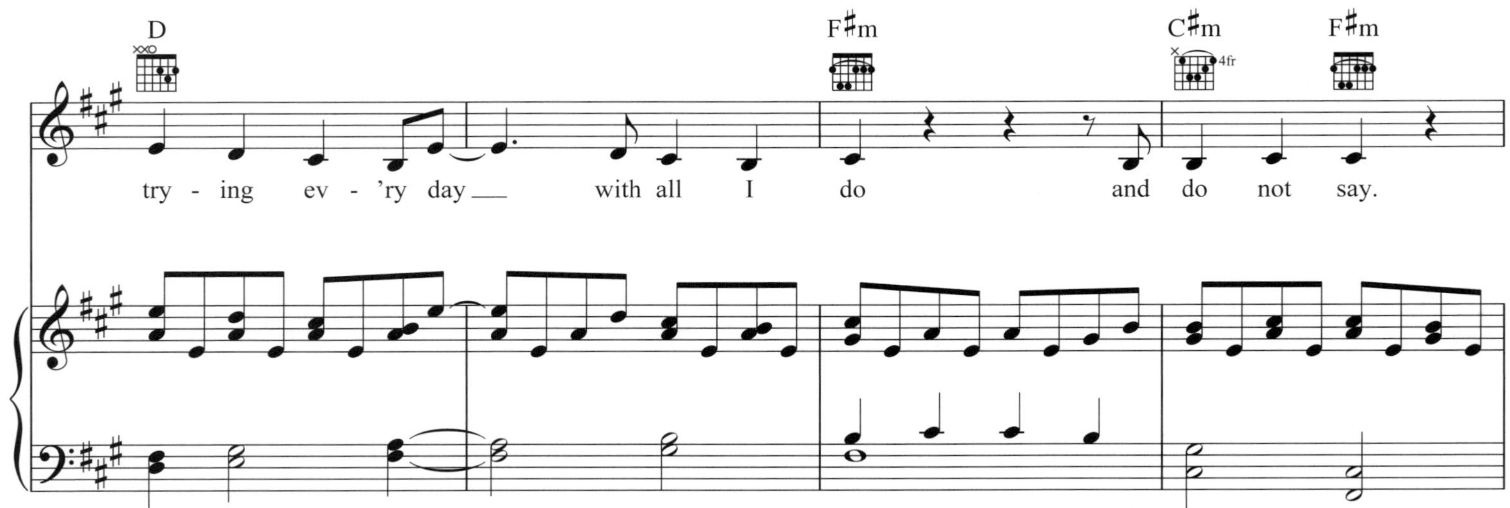

A/D
C#m
4fr
Here, on the edge of the a - byss, know - ing
Bm
F#m
ev - 'ry - thing in my whole life has led to this.
D
E
And so I pull in - side my - self, close the walls, put up my guard.
mf
F#m
E
E/D
I prac - tice ev - 'ry sin - gle day for this, so why is it so

Bm
A/E
hard?
'Cause I can't show you I'm not as
Em7
D
Dm(add2)
5fr
cold as I seem. There are things you can-not know, and it's
mp
F♯m
Bm
B♭
B♭m
A/E
dan - ger - ous to dream.
C♯m
4fr
I know I'll nev-er see that sun-ny day when this
mf

D
F♯m
C♯m
F♯m
4fr
trial is fi - n'lly through
and it could just be me and you.
A/D
C♯m
4fr
I can't dwell on what we've lost
and how
Bm
F♯m
se - cre - cy and si - lence comes at such a cost.
Dmaj7
E
I wish I could tell the truth, show you who's be - hind the door.

F♯m
E
E/D
I wish you knew what all this pan - to-mime and pag - eant-ry was
Bm
A/E
for. I have to be so cau - tious and
Em7
D
Dm(add2)
5fr
you're so ex - treme. We're dif - f'rent, you and I. And it's
3
3
mp
Faster
F♯m/A
Bm
B♭
A
dan - ger - ous to dream. It's
cresc.

G
D
F
G/C
dan - ger - ous to wish I could make choic - es of my own.
f
E♭
3fr
E♭/B♭
6fr
Fm/A♭
Dan - ger - ous to e - ven have that thought. I'm
C/G
Dm/G
B/G
Dm/F
dan - ger - ous just stand - ing here for ev - 'ry - one to see. If
Meno mosso
A/E
A/F
Dmaj7
I let go of rules, who knows how dan - ger - ous I'd

C♯7
N.C./C♯
ELSA:
be?
BISHOP: Your majesty, the gloves.
Why right now would I make
rit.
colla voce
8vb

this mis- take?
How could I let my con - cen - tra - tion break?
(8vb)

With movement
ELSA: Conceal...don't feel...conceal...don't feel...
cresc.

BISHOP: Sem hon heldr inum helgum eignum ok krýnd í þessum helga stað ek té fram fyrir yðr... Queen Elsa of Arendelle.
f
rit.

Maestoso
A
C♯m
4fr
WOMEN:
Queen a - noint - ed, our cho - sen daugh - ter, our
MEN:
Queen a - noint - ed, our cho - sen daugh - ter, our
ff
3
3
Fast Waltz
D
A/E
E
bless - ed queen be - hold.
bless - ed queen be - hold.
cresc.
C
Em
F
8va

E
8va
G♯m
4fr
(8va)
A
Flowing, as before
A/E
dim.
p sub.
ELSA:
C♯m
4fr
I can't be - lieve I'm stand - ing here. Did I
D
F♯m
real - ly make it through? _ Fa - ther, I did it! Now what
3

C♯m
F♯m
A/D
C♯m
4fr
do I do?
I can't stop smil - ing;
how ___ strange!
mp
Bm
F♯m
Does this mean that things are dif - f'rent?
Could they real - ly change?
Dmaj7
E
And could I o - pen up ___ that door ___ and fi - n'lly
F♯m
E
see you face to face? ___
I guess a queen ___ can change ___ the rules ___ but not ___ the rea -

E/D
Bm
A(add2)
- sons they're in place.
I can't be what you ex-
Em7(add4)
5fr
D(add2)
Dm
pect of me, and I'm not what I seem, but I would love to
Freely
F♯m/A
Bm
F
know you. Is it dan - ger - ous to dream?
colla voce
Flowing
A/E
Dmaj9
4fr
Dm6
A
mp
cresc.
rit.
f

LOVE IS AN OPEN DOOR

Music and Lyrics by KRISTEN ANDERSON-LOPEZ
and ROBERT LOPEZ

D/G
Dsus/A
D
Dsus/F♯
Dsus/E
Dsus/A
ANNA:
But with you,
find my own place, and may-be it's the par-ty talk-ing, or the choc-'late fon-due.
Bm
D
Am/D
E7
I see your face, and it's noth-ing like I've ev-er known be-
But with you, I found my place, and it's noth-ing like I've ev-er known be-
Gm7
D
Dmaj9/F♯
E7
Gm7
fore. Love is an o-pen door! Love is an o-pen
fore. Love is an o-pen door! Love is an o-pen
f
sim.

D
Dmaj9/F♯
E7
Gm7
D
Dmaj9/F♯
door! ___ Love is an o - pen door! With you! With
door! ___ Love is an o - pen door! With you!
E7
Gm7
D
Dsus/F♯
D/G
Dsus/A
you! Love is an o - pen door.
With you! Love is an o - pen door.
mp
D
Dsus/F♯
G
D/G
G/A
3fr
Dsus/A
HANS:
I mean it's
6

E
Esus/G♯
E/A
Esus/B
What? Sand - wich - es. I've nev - er
cra - zy, we fin - ish each oth - er's. That's what I was gon - na say!
mf
E
Esus/G♯
Esus/F♯
Esus/B
met some - one who thinks so much like me. Jinx. Jinx a - gain. Our
Who thinks so much like me. Jinx. Jinx a - gain. Our
sim.
E
Esus/G♯
E/G♯
E/A
Esus/B
men - tal syn - chro - ni - za - tion can have but one ex - pla - na - tion:
men - tal syn - chro - ni - za - tion can have but one ex - pla - na - tion:

E
Esus/G♯
E/F♯
Esus/B
C♯m
4fr
and I, just meant to be.
Say good - bye to the pain
you were meant to be.
Say good-bye to the pain
E
Bm/E
F♯7
Am7
of the past.
We don't have to feel it an - y - more!
Love is an o - pen
of the past.
We don't have to feel it an - y - more!
Love is an o - pen
sim.
E
Emaj9/G♯
F♯7
Am7
E
Emaj9/G♯
door!
Love is an o - pen
door!
door!
Love is an o - pen
door!
f

F♯7 Am7 E Emaj9/G♯ F♯7 Am7
Life can be so much more! With you! With you! Love is an o - pen
Life can be so much more! With you! With you! Love is an o - pen
E Esus/G♯ Esus/F♯ Esus/B E Esus/G♯
door.
door.
HANS: Can I say something crazy? Will you marry me?
f dim.
mp
A E/A A/B Esus/B N.C. C5 C9
3fr
ANNA:
ANNA: Can I just say something crazier? Yes.
Love is an o - pen
HANS:
Love is an o - pen
mf f

F
Fmaj9/A
G7
B♭m7
door! Love is an o - pen door!
door! Love is an o - pen door!
Life can be so much more! With you! With you!
Life can be so much more! With you! With you!
Love is an o - pen door!
Love is an o - pen door!

WHAT DO YOU KNOW ABOUT LOVE?

Music and Lyrics by KRISTEN ANDERSON-LOPEZ
and ROBERT LOPEZ

F7
C/G
G
Fsus2
F5
ANNA:
Some peo - ple know their hearts the min - ute true love starts.
KRISTOFF:
O - kay, you fright - en me.
3
Am
G
F
C/G
G
ANNA: I like books.
Some peo - ple sim - ply know
KRISTOFF:
Some peo - ple read a lot of books.
Fsus2
F5
Dm7
C/E
F
G/F
F
G
when true love says, "Hel - lo!"
Some folks are tak - en in by cur - ly locks and prince - ly looks.

A bit brighter
ANNA: He does have princely looks, we agree on that one!
C7
F/C
F7
B♭/F
KRISTOFF: Right! By the way, what color eyes does he have?
C7
F/C
E7
E7sus
A7
D/A
D7
G/D
A7
D/A
KRISTOFF:
All I'm say'n is when you go to climb a moun - tain, you don't just jump to the top.
sim.
8vb
D7
G/D
A7
D/A
D7
G/D
ANNA:
If it's true love, you can!
There's scal - in' and scram - blin' and too man-y steps for count - in'
(8vb)

A7
D/A
D
A/E
E
KRISTOFF:
KRISTOFF:
and the work does-n't stop.
ANNA: Maybe for YOU.
Love's not an eas - y climb,
(8vb)
Dsus2
D5
5fr
F#m
E
D
A/E
ANNA:
We get a whole life, that's the plan.
you have to take your time.
KRISTOFF: That's not a plan.
E
Dsus2
D5
5fr
Bm
F#m/C#
So says a sweat-y, smell-y
Love's not a thing you get,
it's work and tears and sweat.

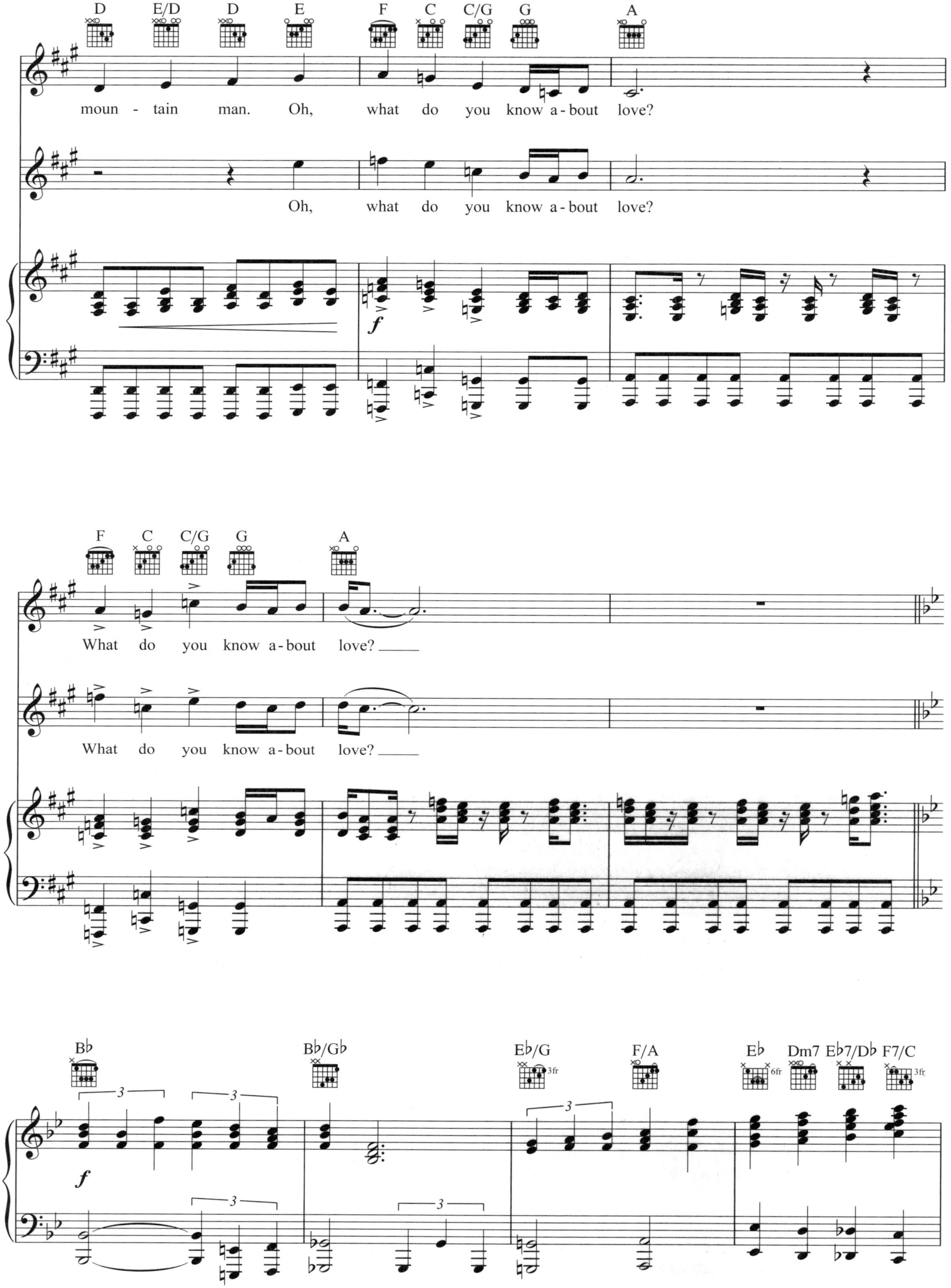

D E/D D E F C C/G G A

mountain man. Oh, what do you know about love?

Oh, what do you know about love?

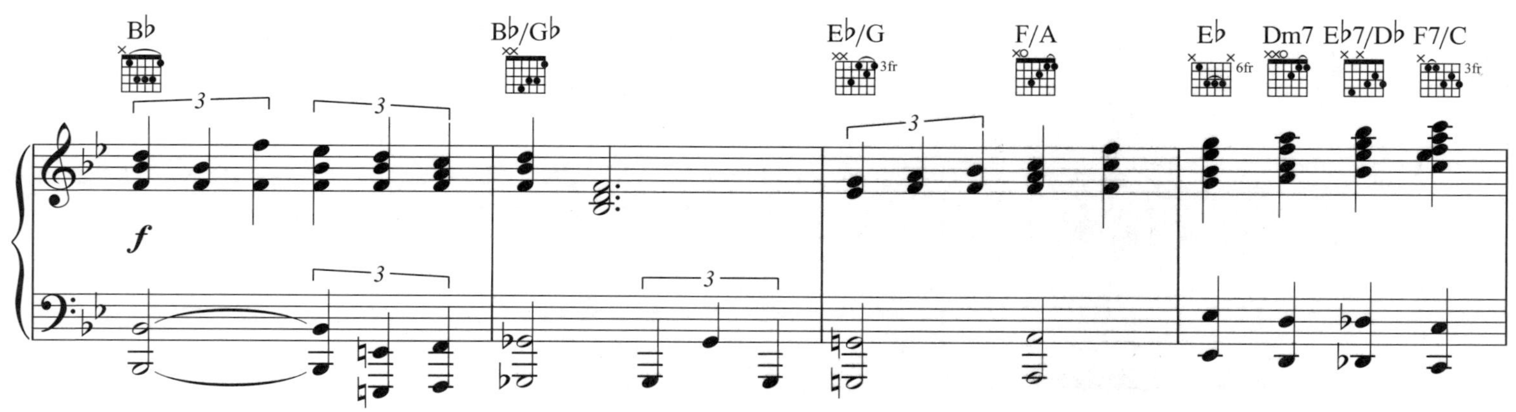

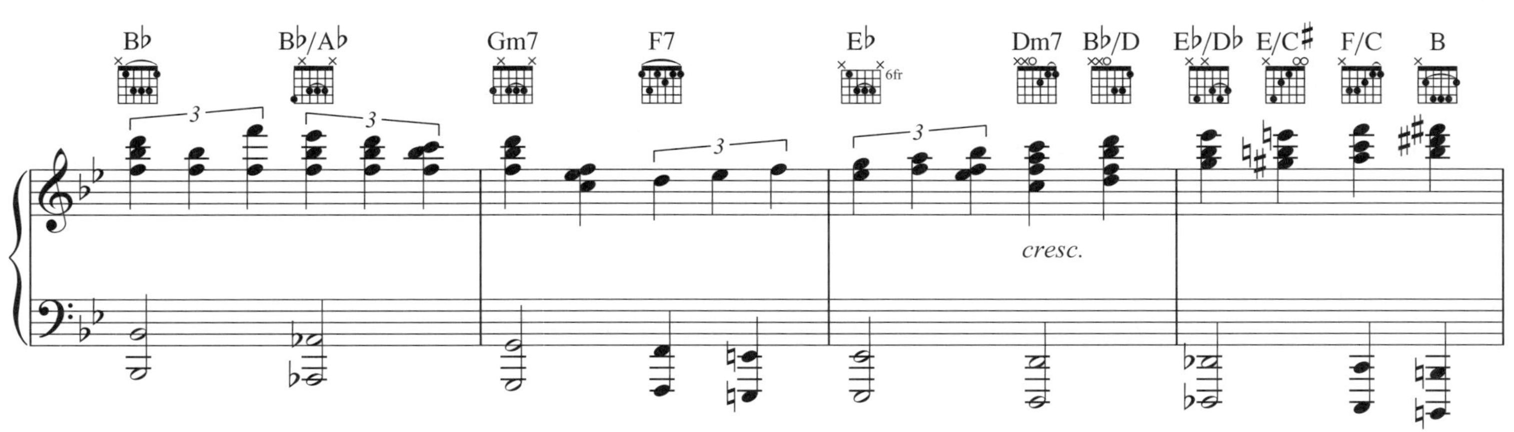
Bb
Bb/Ab
Gm7
F7
Eb
Dm7
Bb/D
Eb/Db
E/C#
F/C
B
cresc.

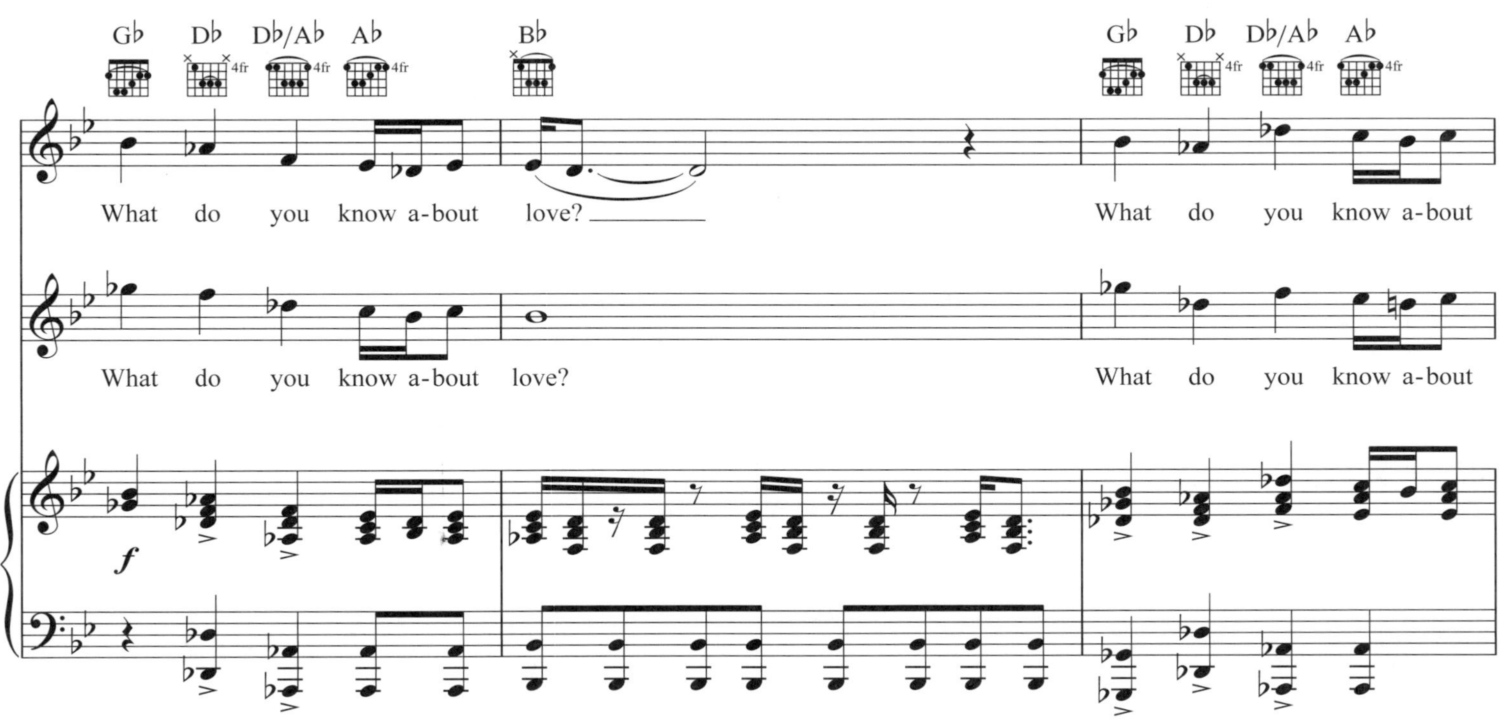
Gb
Db
Db/Ab
Ab
Bb
What do you know a-bout love?
What do you know a-bout
What do you know a-bout love?
What do you know a-bout
f

Bb
Ebm
Db
Abm/Cb
love?
Have you e-ven kissed a girl?
I mean a hu-man girl!
love?
Oh.

G♭ D♭ D♭/A♭ A♭ B♭ Gm7
4fr 4fr 4fr
What do you know a-bout an-y-thing? An-y - thing?
What do you know a-bout an-y-thing? An-y - thing? An-y - one with half a brain _ would-'ve worn _
A♭maj7 Gm7 A♭maj9 F7
3fr
An-y - one _ with half a life _ would have one friend who's not a deer.
_ some win-ter gear! I
B♭ Gm7 A♭maj9
3fr
An - y fool _
do. An - y fool _ who jumps head - long _ is gon - na bang their head. _

KRISTOFF: Aaah!
Gbmaj7/F Ab/Gb Bb/Ab Gb/Bb Ab/C Cb/Db Bb5/F Bb
who does-n't jump right now is prob-'ly gon-na end up dead! Like I said.
Eb/F F
Slower, with effort
Gb/F F/F# F#/G Ab/A
More freely
Bb Eb Bb7
ANNA:
I'd like to point out that we've come a good long way here, and that you're, wow, real-ly
mf
Eb Bb7 Eb
strong.
KRISTOFF:
I lift a lot of ice. You saved my life just now, I guess I got-ta say here

B♭7
E♭
F
And see? You're nice!
my first im - pres - sion was wrong.
That jump was real - ly brave.
E♭sus2
Gm
F
E♭(add2)
Your catch was quite a save!
You've got some brains.
You've got some guts.
Thanks.
Fsus2
F
Fsus/E♭
With miles and miles to go,
I guess it's nice to know
With miles and miles to go,
I guess it's nice to know
mp

Cm7
B♭/D
E♭
F
that I can trust you. Though the ques - tion still re - mains.
that I can trust you. Though the ques - tion still re - mains.
rit.
Moving into tempo
KRISTOFF: Just be careful.
G♭
D♭/A♭
A♭
B♭
What do you know a - bout love?
What do you know a - bout
What do you know a - bout love?
What do you know a - bout
ANNA: Have a little faith.
Tempo I
E♭m
D♭
C♭
love?
At least we know one thing.
This trip should be in - t'rest - ing.
love?
At least we know one thing.
This trip should be in - t'rest - ing.
f

Gb
Db
Db/Ab
Ab
Bb
4fr
4fr
4fr
What do you know a - bout love?
What do you know a - bout love?
Gb
Db/Gb
Db/Ab
4fr
4fr
What do you know a - bout
What do you know a - bout
Bb
Fm7
A/F
Bb
love?
love?

IN SUMMER

Music and Lyrics by KRISTEN ANDERSON-LOPEZ
and ROBERT LOPEZ

Emaj13
7fr
A6/9
sum - mer.
I'll fi - n'lly see a sum - mer breeze blow a -
E(add2)
C♯m
4fr
F♯9
3fr
A6
G♯m
4fr
F♯m7
way a win - ter storm
and find out what hap - pens to sol - id wa - ter when it gets warm.
B9sus
5fr
E6
F♯m9
2fr
Emaj7/G♯
Am6
And I can't wait to see what my bud - dies all think of me. Just i -
G7
C♯m7
4fr
F9
B13
7fr
Emaj13
7fr
C6/9
mag - ine how much cool - er I'll be in sum - mer!
Da

F6/9
Gm7
F6/9
Gm7
Am7
da da doo ba ba ba ba ba-ba boo.
The hot and the cold are both so in-tense.
f
D7
Gm7
C13
2fr
F6/9
Gm9
3fr
Am7
G9♭5
Put 'em to-geth-er, it just makes sense!
Rat da dat da da da da da da da doo.
8va
Gm(add2)/B♭
A7
Dm
G
B♭/C
Win-ter's a good time to stay in and cud-dle, but put me in sum-mer and I'll be a— Hap-py snow-man!
B♭6/9
F(add2)
When life gets rough I like to hold on to my dream of re-
mp legato

Dm
G9
9fr
B♭6
Am
Gm7
C9sus
lax - ing in the sum-mer sun just let-ting off steam! Oh the
p
Slower
Fmaj13
B♭6/9
Fmaj13
B♭m6/D♭
2fr
sky will be blue, and you guys-'ll be there too, when I
G♯7
4fr
Dm7
F♯9
3fr
C13
2fr
F
N.C.
fi-nal-ly do what fro-zen things do in sum-mer!
a tempo
p
N.C./C
F(add2)
In sum-mer!

HANS OF THE SOUTHERN ISLES
(Reprise)

Music and Lyrics by KRISTEN ANDERSON-LOPEZ
and ROBERT LOPEZ

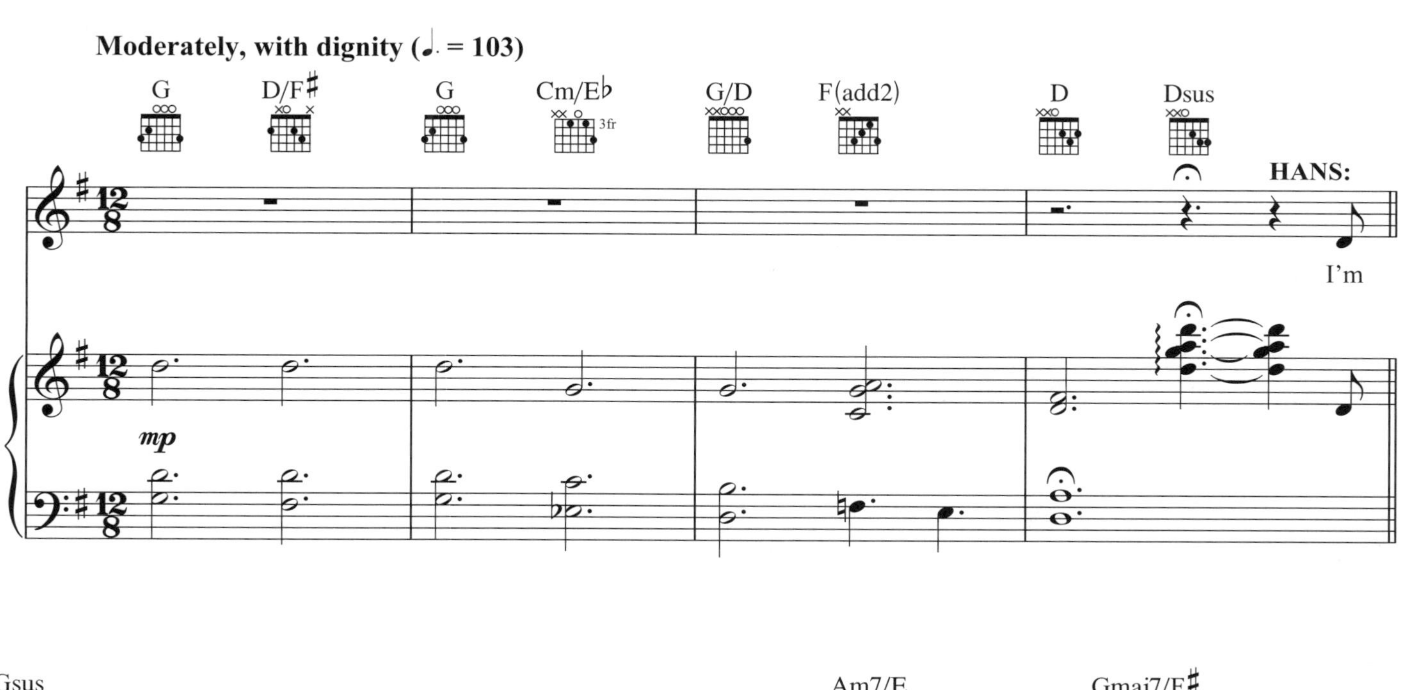

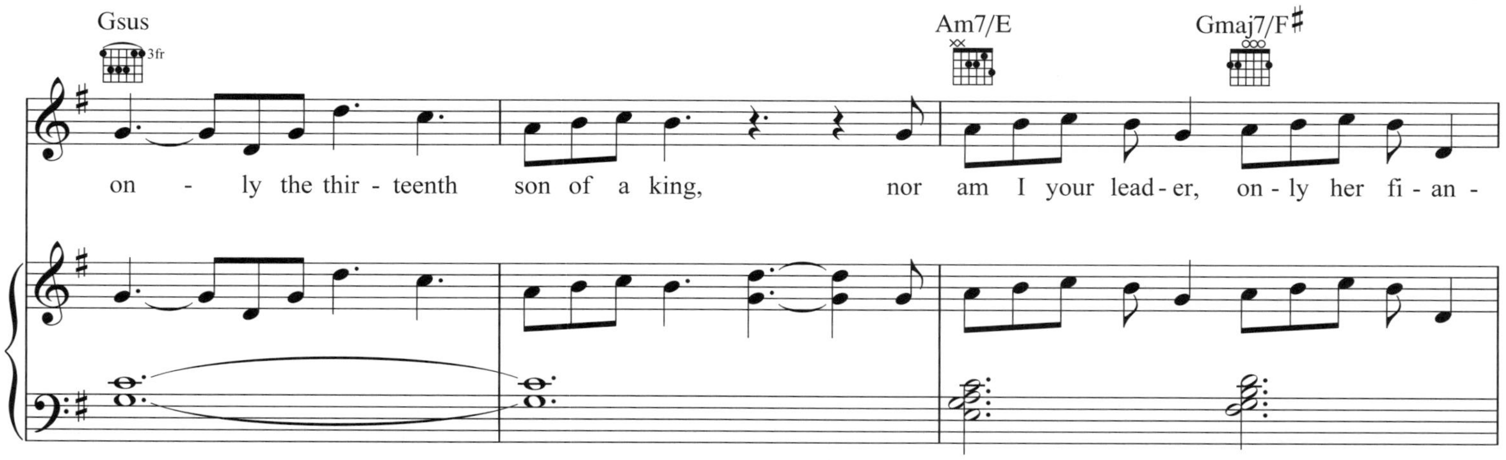

Cm/E♭
G/D
D7sus
Gsus
G
3fr
give in to fear, not here, not to - day. We
Più mosso
C
G/B
F/A
G/B
C
Dm
Am
can't know how threat-'ning the road a - head will be, but put your faith in An - na, the
B♭
F
Asus
A
Freely
Dm
way that An - na put her faith in me. I can't tell you what your prin - cess
mp colla voce
B♭sus2
F(add2)
Am/E
D
sees in me, but let me tell you what an hon - or it would be if
poco rit.
mf

G
F/G
C
you could let me lead you through this time of trials. You
rit.
f
Faster (♩. = 116)
G
G/F
C/E
Cm/E♭
3fr
G/D
D7sus
ask for a leader, a servant responds. Trust Hans of the Southern
mf
March-like
G5
3fr
♩. = ♩
D5
5fr
C/E
D/F♯
TENOR:
Isles. He's more than the thirteenth
mp
f
G
D/F♯
G
Cm/E♭
3fr
G/D
SOPRANO :
son of a king. We're lucky he came along in our time of

F C/E D G/B Csus2 D Em Cm6/E♭
3fr
need.
WOMEN:
Let's lis-ten to
MEN:
We'll nev - er give in to fear or to trea-son.
G/D D7 C5/G G C G
3fr
HANS:
WESELTON:
Who will come with me? My
rea-son and fol - low his lead.
and fol - low his lead.
F/A G/B C Dm Am B♭ F
men and I, my lord! Yes, We-sel-ton a-ris-es and of-fers up the pow-er of his
mf

Esus
Asus
Dsus
D
G/B
Csus2
3fr
HANS:
sword.
I call to your king-dom.
WOMEN:
Our
MEN:
Our
cresc.
D
Em
Cm6/E♭
G/D
Dsus
Cm/D
3fr
king-dom re-sponds to Hans. Fol-low Hans, Prince Hans of the
to Hans! It's Hans!
king-dom re-sponds to Hans. Fol-low Hans, Prince Hans of the
G
A♭maj7/D♭
4fr
G
South - ern Isles!
South - ern Isles!
8va

LET IT GO

Music and Lyrics by KRISTEN ANDERSON-LOPEZ
and ROBERT LOPEZ

D(add2)
Asus
A
Em
looks like I'm the queen. The wind is howl -
Cmaj7
D(add2)
Asus
Am
- ing like this swirl - ing storm in - side.
Em
D
A
Could - n't keep it in, heav - en knows I tried.
D
Don't let them in, don't let them see.
mf

C
D
Be the good girl you al - ways have to be. Con - ceal. Don't feel.
C
Don't let them know. Well, now
cresc.
G
they know. Let it go, let it go.
mf
D
Em
C
Can't hold it back an - y - more. Let it go,

G
D
Em
let it go.
Turn a - way and slam the door.
C
G
D
I don't care what they're
Em
C
Bm
going to say.
Let the storm rage on.
B♭
C5
3fr
The cold nev - er both-ered me an - y - way.

G
D/F♯
Em
It's fun - ny how some dis -
sim.
C
D
Am
- tance makes ev - 'ry - thing seem small. and the
Em
D
Asus
A
fears that once con - trolled me can't get to me at all.
D
C
It's time to see what I can do,
sim.

D
to test the lim - its and break through. No right, no wrong,
C
no rules for me. I'm free!
G
D
Let it go! Let it go! I am one
Em
C
G
D
with the wind and sky. Let it go! Let it go!
f

Em
C
You'll nev - er see me cry.
G
D
Em
C
Here I stand, and here I'll stay. Let the
Bm
B♭
C5
3fr
storm rage on.
ff

My pow - er flur - ries through the air in - to the ground.
My soul is spi - ral - ing in fro - zen frac - tals all a - round.
D5
5fr
And one thought crys - tal - liz - es like an i - cy blast.

E
Cmaj7
D
Am
I'm nev - er go - ing back, the past is in the past!
ff
mf
C
G
D
Let it go! Let it go! And I'll rise
ff
f
Em
C
G
D
like the break - of dawn Let it go! Let it go!
Em
C
That per - fect girl is gone.

G
D
Em
C
Here I stand in the light of day.
Cm/G
Bm
B♭
3fr
Let the storm rage on!
cresc.
C5
3fr
The cold nev - er both - ered me an - y - way!
mf
B♭
C
D
ff
rall.

HYGGE

Music and Lyrics by KRISTEN ANDERSON-LOPEZ
and ROBERT LOPEZ

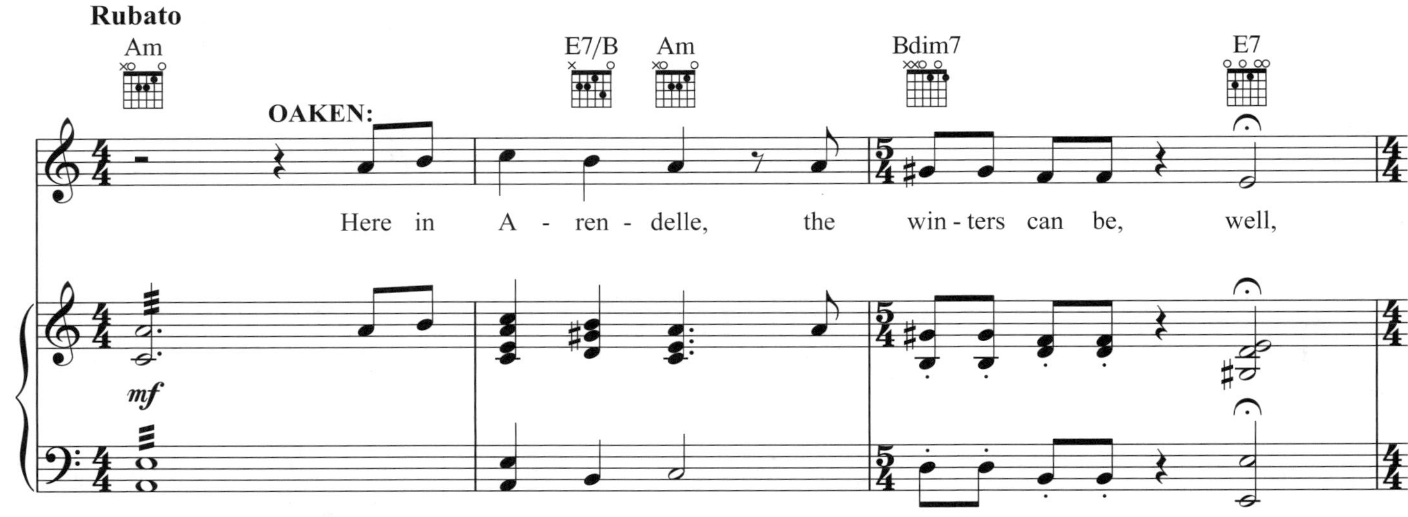

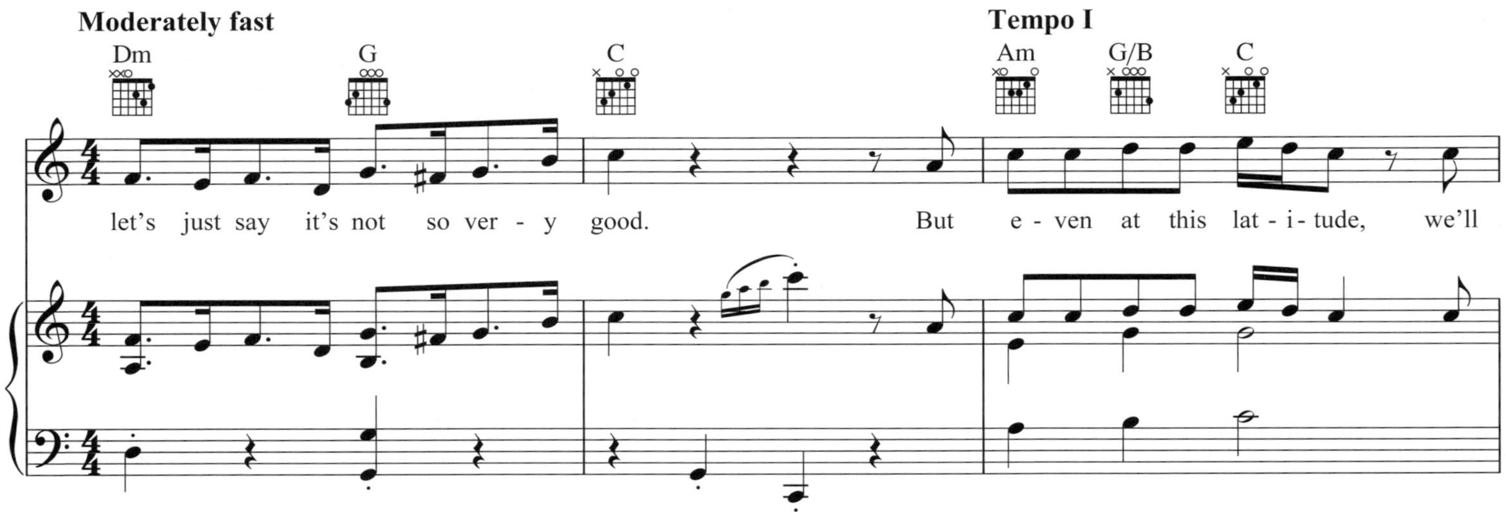

*Pronounced "hue-gah"

A6
A6/E
E9
E9/B
Hy - gge hy - gge hy - gge hy - gge hy - gge hy - gge hy - gge hy - gge hy - gge hy - gge hy - gge hy - gge.
f
E9
Hy - gge - li hy - gge - li hy - gge - li hy - gge - li hy - gge - li hy - gge - li. I will trans - late
Faster
A
A6
A6/E
A6
more. Hy - gge means
D/A
E9
can - dle - light, hy - gge means eas - y, hy - gge means

E7
N.C.
A7
all to-geth-er play-ing how you say? Par - chee - si.
mf
Dm7
G
C
B
C
Find - ing a spi - der in your shoe? Not hy - gge.
F♯m7♭5
4fr
B
F7
E
D♯
6fr
E
Hav - ing an an - noy - ing thing to do? Not hy - gge!
A6
Dm6
Hy - gge's not sched - u - led, you can't say when it starts or ends.
mf

A/E F♯m7 Bm Bm7♭5 Dm6/F E+ A

(not pitched)

Most im - por - tant - ly, it can't be hy - gge with - out your fam - i - ly and friends! Oh,

WOMEN:

Oh,

MEN:

A6 A6/E E9 E9/B

Hy - gge hy - gge hy - gge hy - gge hy - gge hy - gge hy - gge hy - gge hy - gge hy - gge hy - gge hy - gge.

Hy - gge hy - gge hy - gge hy - gge hy - gge hy - gge hy - gge hy - gge hy - gge hy - gge hy - gge hy - gge.

E9
A6
N.C.
Hy-gge-li hy-gge-li hy-gge-li hy-gge-li hy-gge-li hy-gge-li. Now it's time to sweat.
hy-gge-li hy-gge-li hy-gge-li. Now it's time to sweat.
sfz
B♭6
OAKEN:
Hy - gge is al - co - hol,
p
E♭6/B♭
F9/A
F+/A
hy - gge is eat - ing, hy - gge is glugg, a - maz - ing

B♭6/9
B♭
stuff when you are need - ing heat - ing. Hy - gge means you're
E♭m6
B♭/F
Gm7
friend - ly. You stop want - ing to be rude. Join us for some su - per -
Cm
Cm7♭5
E♭m6/G♭
F
F+
B♭/F
du - per hy - gge in the sau - na in the nude!
3fr
4fr
WOMEN:
Oh,
MEN:

B♭6 B♭6/F

OAKEN:

Don't wor-ry a-bout your bod-y, noth-ing we have-n't seen.

Hy-gge hy-gge hy-gge hy-gge hy-gge hy-gge.

f

F9 F9/C

Whip your-self with a branch and you will feel nice and clean!

Hy-gge hy-gge hy-gge hy-gge hy-gge hy-gge.

F9
Go on, get in the sau - na!
Hy-gge - li hy - gge - li hy - gge - li.
Hy-gge - li hy - gge - li hy - gge - li.
F+
N.C.
Come on, you know you waun - na!
Now it's time to drink!
A♭7
D♭
B♭m
WOMEN:
to
OAKEN:
A ___ toast to all our fam - i - ly and friends;
add MEN:
to

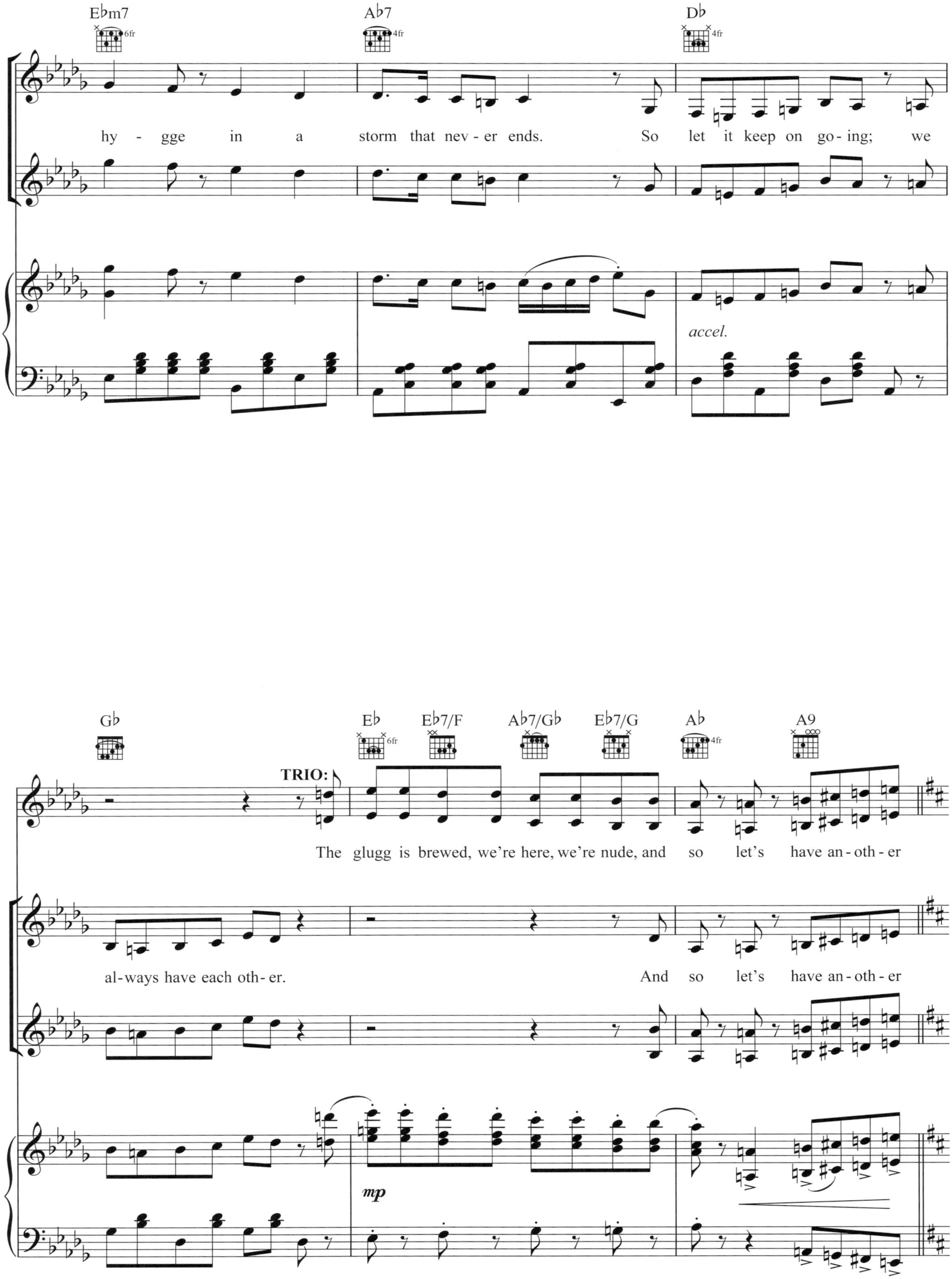

G♭ E♭ 6fr E♭7/F A♭7/G♭ E♭7/G A♭ 4fr A9

TRIO:

The glugg is brewed, we're here, we're nude, and so let's have an - oth - er

al - ways have each oth - er. And so let's have an - oth - er

mp

D
Bm
Em7
Ha
Ha ha ha ha ha ha ha ha ha ha ha ha
Ha ha ha ha ha ha ha ha ha ha ha ha ha ha
toast to all our fam - i - ly and friends; to hy - gge in a
A
D
G
F7
The
ha ha ha ha ha ha ha ha ha ha ha. The
ha ha ha ha ha ha ha ha ha ha ha ha ha. The
storm that nev - er ends. So let it keep on go - ing. We al - ways have each oth - er. The

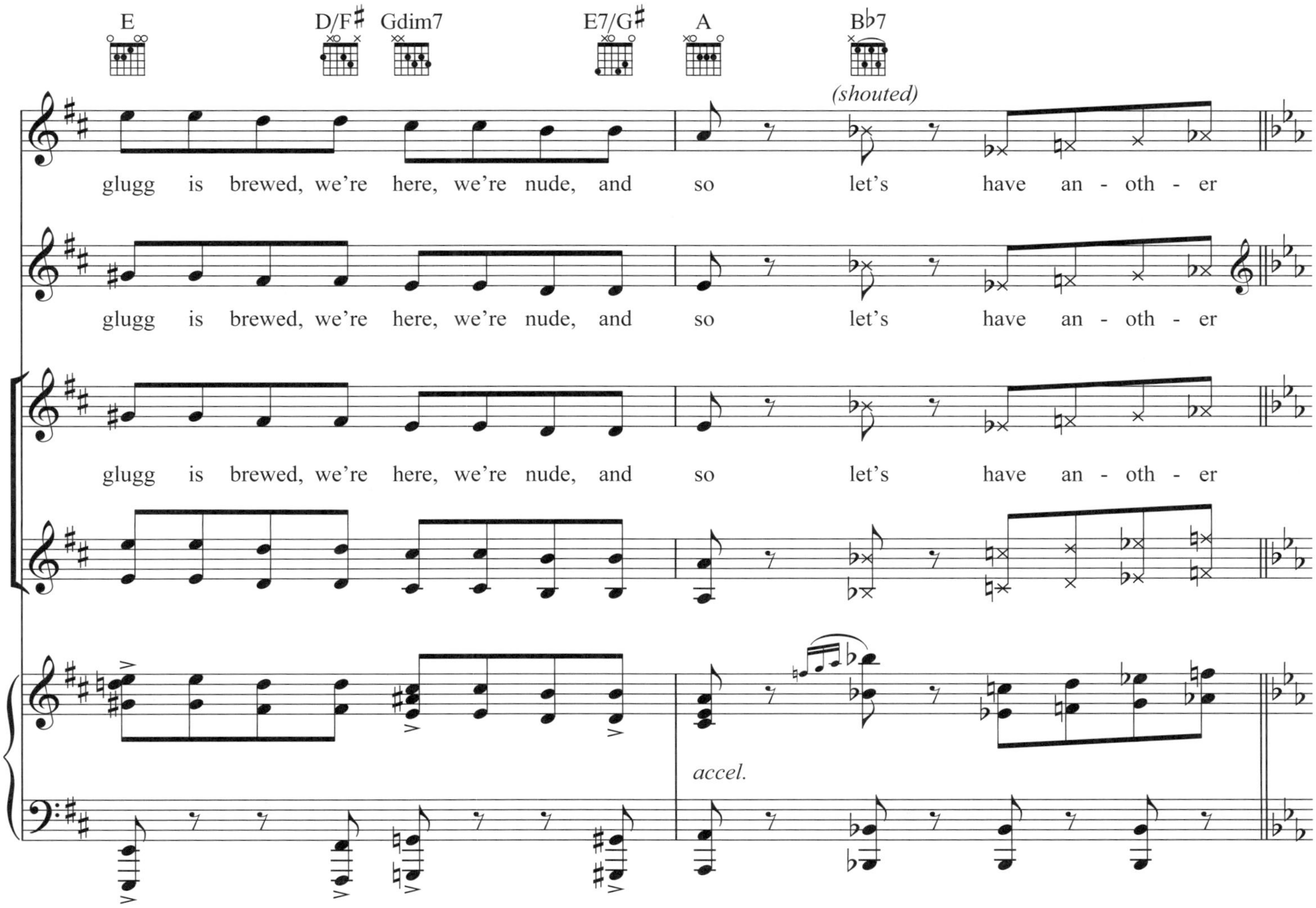
E D/F♯ Gdim7 E7/G♯ A B♭7
(shouted)
glugg is brewed, we're here, we're nude, and so let's have an - oth - er
glugg is brewed, we're here, we're nude, and so let's have an - oth - er
glugg is brewed, we're here, we're nude, and so let's have an - oth - er
accel.

E♭ B♭ E♭ B♭ Cm Fm C Fm F7(no3rd)
6fr 6fr 3fr 3fr
(WOMEN)
Hi - ya hi - ya hi - ya Hi - ya hi - ya
(MEN)
toast to all our fam - i - ly and friends; to hy - gge in a

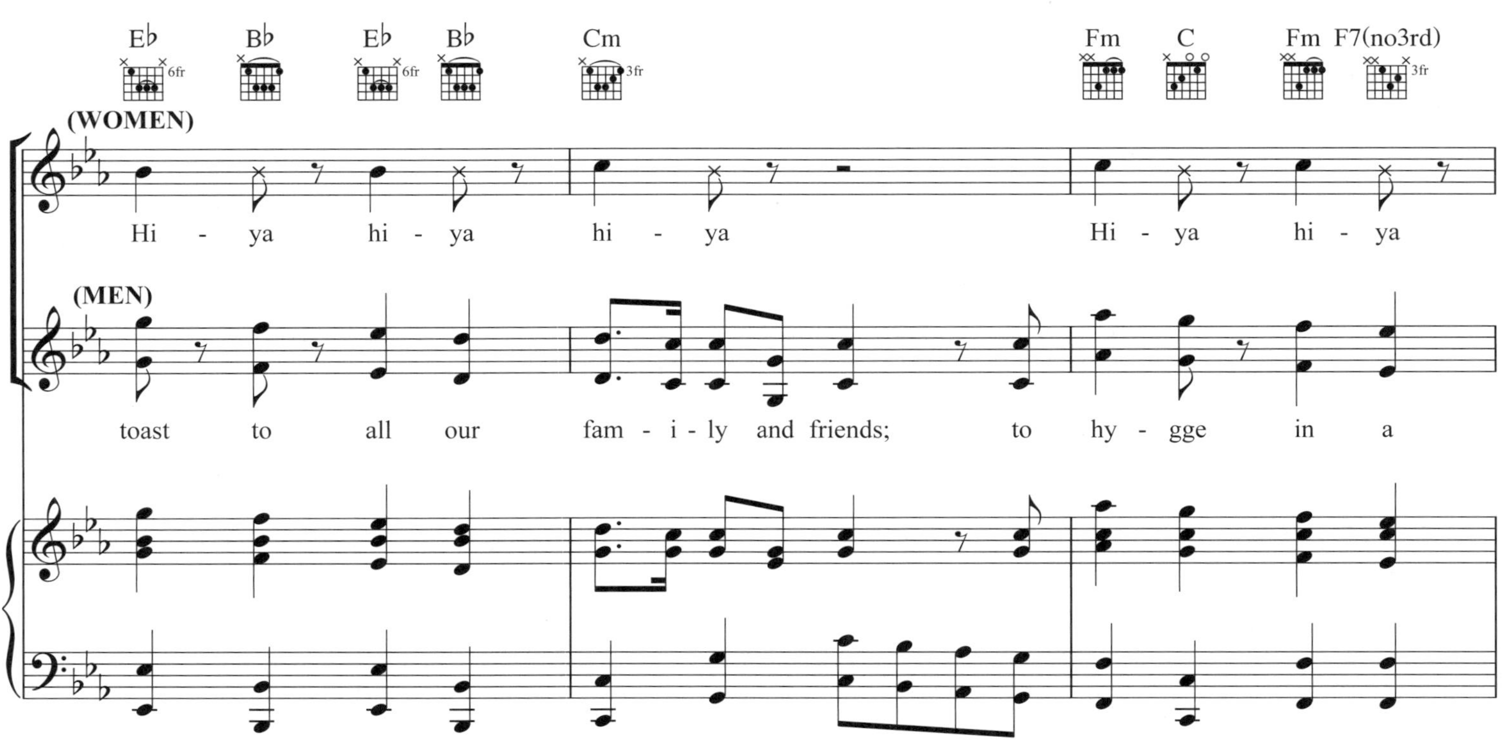

B♭
E♭/G
A♭
hi - ya. Hi - ya hi - ya hi - ya. The
storm that nev - er ends. So let it keep on go - ing; we al - ways have each oth - er. The
F7
E♭/G
A♭dim7
F7/A
B7
KRISTOFF:
Ex - CUSE ME!
glugg is brewed, we're here, we're nude, and so...
Slower
Dm7
G
C
B
C
Starv - ing to death with - in a week? A
MEN & WOMEN:
Not hy - gge.
mp

F♯m7♭5
B
F7
E
D♯
E
ANNA:
fu - ture that's cold and dead and bleak?
He's
Not hy - gge!
A
A9/C♯
D
Dm6/F
A6/E
OAKEN:
right, we have to go. We have an ur-gent job to do.
If you can't stay here with
legato
poco rit.
p colla voce
Folksy Waltz
F♯7
Bm
E7
A
us to hy - gge, take all the hy - gge that you can with you!
WOMEN:
Oh,
MEN:
f

A6 A6/E

N.C.

OAKEN: Co-zi-est cloak and dress and boots! ANNA: Thanks!

Hy-gge hy-gge hy-gge hy-gge hy-gge hy-gge.

mf

E9 E9/B

N.C.

OAKEN: One of our skimp-i-est swim-ming suits! OLAF: Yes!

Hy-gge hy-gge hy-gge hy-gge hy-gge hy-gge.

E
D/F♯
Gdim7
E5
Adim7
A♯dim7
WOMEN & MEN:
Hy - gge - li hy - gge - li hy - gge - li hy - gge - li hy - gge - li hy - gge - li.
E7
Edim7
E7
Dm6/F
OAKEN:
You need this rope and this axe! And al - so, you need to re - lax!
p subito
B7/F♯
E♯dim7
B7/F♯
F♯dim7
Please take this sweat - er I knit - ted, and son, if I may be per - mit - ted,
C♯m/G♯
G♯7
A♯dim
heed my ad - vice! I don't need to say twice. You're a - bout to go out on a death march of ice!
cresc.

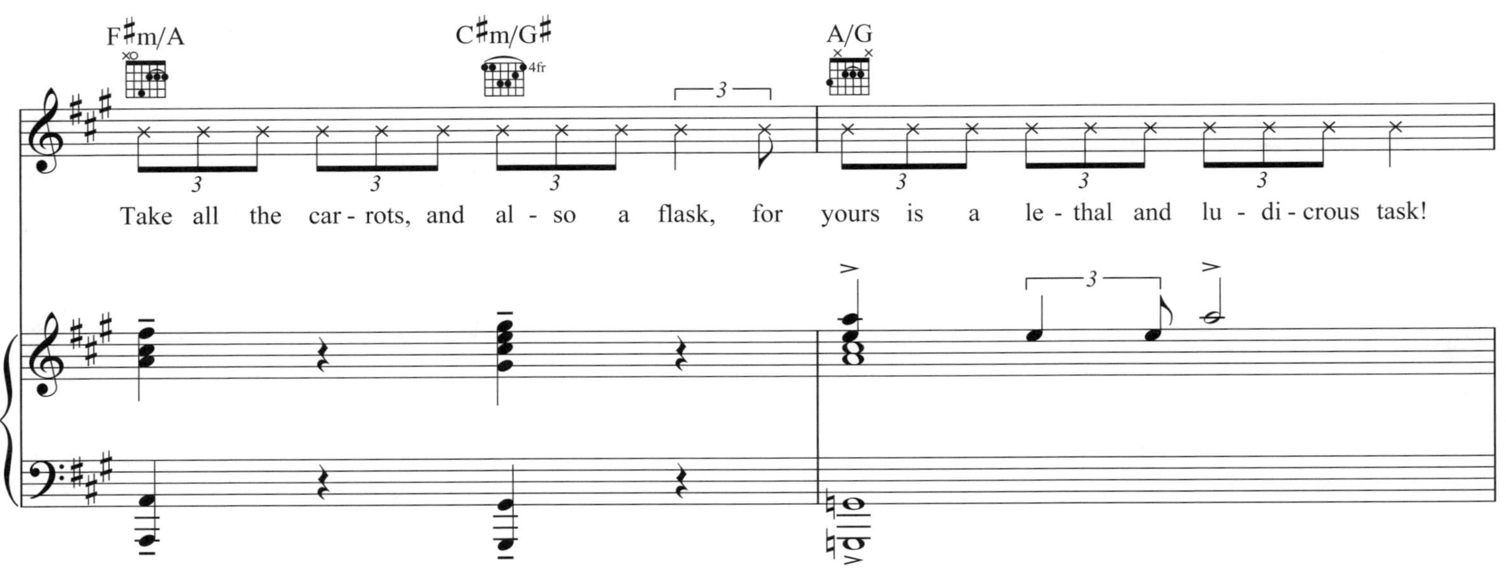
F♯m/A
C♯m/G♯
4fr
A/G
Take all the car - rots, and al - so a flask, for yours is a le - thal and lu - di - crous task!

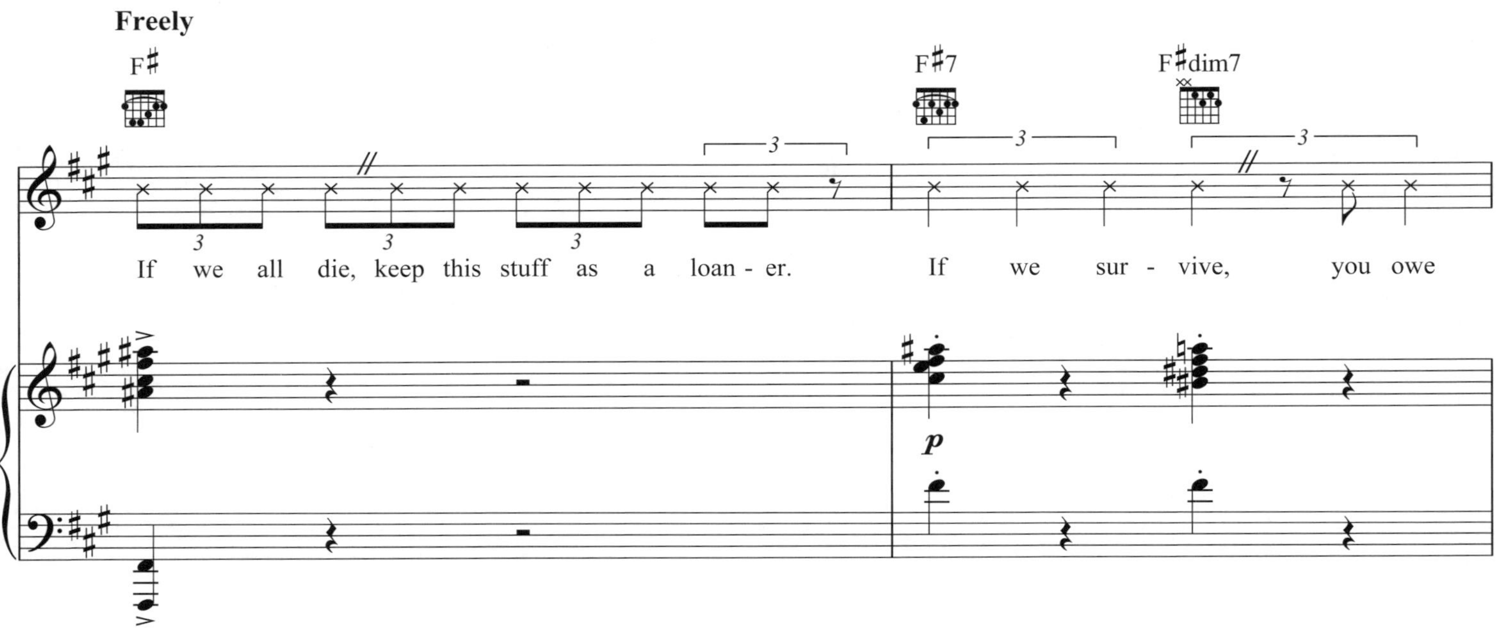
Freely
F♯
F♯7
F♯dim7
If we all die, keep this stuff as a loan - er. If we sur - vive, you owe
p

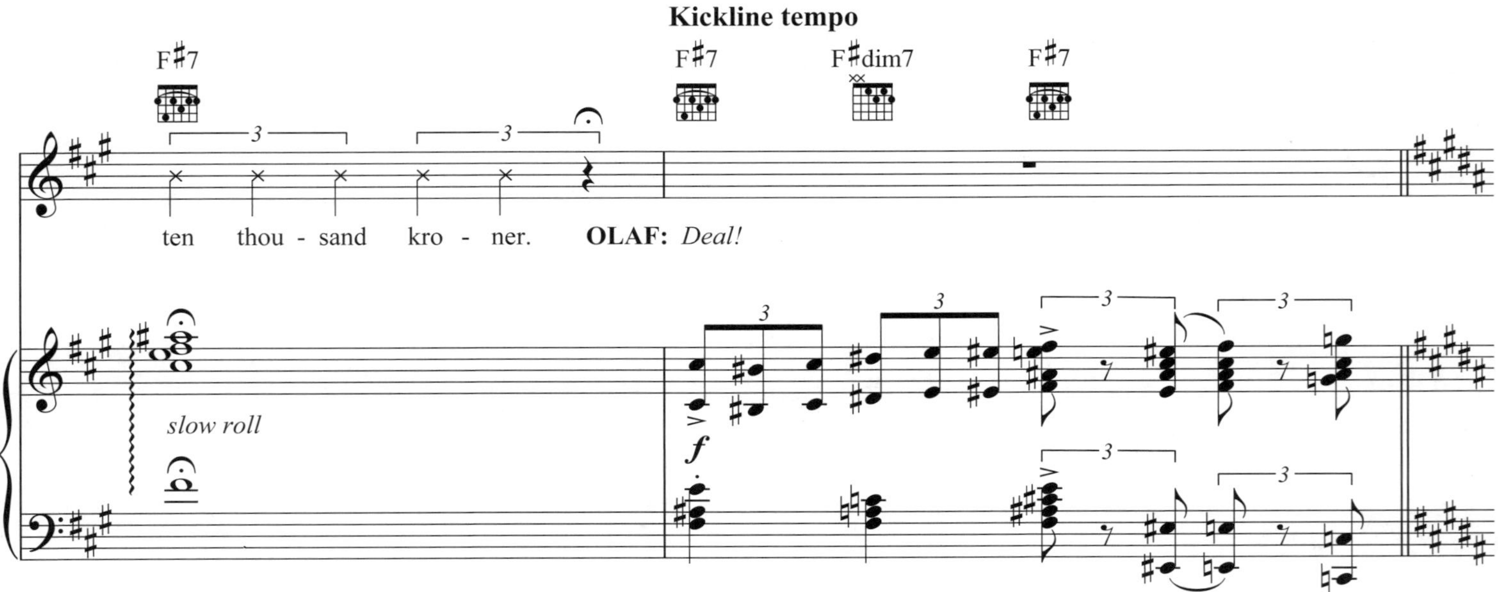
Kickline tempo
F♯7
F♯7
F♯dim7
F♯7
ten thou - sand kro - ner. OLAF: Deal!
slow roll
f

Swing 8ths
B6
C♯m7
4fr
WOMEN:
Hy - gge hy - gge hy - gge hy - gge hy - gge hy - gge hy - gge
MEN:
F♯9
3fr
E/F♯
F♯7
F♯dim7
F♯7
G♭/A♭
A♭7
4fr
G♭/A♭
hy - gge hy - gge hy - gge.
D♭6
A♭9♯5
4fr
D♭6
E♭m7
6fr
A♭9
4fr
E♭m7
6fr
A♭9
4fr
ff

Faster double-time feel, straight 8ths
Gb6/Ab
Ab7
Fm7
Bb
WOMEN:
Ah, ___ ah. ___
MEN:
mf
Eb6
Cm7
Fm7
Bb7
Hy - gge hy - gge hy - gge hy - gge hy-gge hy - gge hy - gge hy - gge hy - gge hy- gge.
Bb
Cb/Bb
C/Bb
Db/Bb
N.C.
Eb
Hy-gge-li hy - gge-li hy-gge-li hy - gge-li hy-gge-li hy - gge-li. WHOO!
sfz

FIXER UPPER
(Broadway Version)

Music and Lyrics by KRISTEN ANDERSON-LOPEZ
and ROBERT LOPEZ

Moderately jaunty
A♭/B♭
B♭
E♭
pear-shaped, square-shaped, weird-ness of his feet?
HIDDEN FOLK 1:
And though we
A♭
D♭
BULDA:
But you'll
know he wash-es well, he al-ways ends up sor-ta smell-y.
Cm
Cm/B♭
B♭
E♭
nev-er meet a fel-la who's as sen-si-tive and sweet.

A♭
G♭/A♭
D♭/A♭
E
E♭
BULDA:
Like his pe-
PABBIE:
So he's a bit of a fix - er up - per, so he's got a few flaws.
A♭
G♭/A♭
D♭/A♭
E♭/A♭
cu-li-ar brain, dear. That's a lit-tle out-side of na - ture's laws.
OLAF:
His thing with the rein - deer, that's a lit-tle out-side of na - ture's laws.
A♭
G♭/A♭
D♭
A♭/C
B♭
But this we're cer-tain of: you can
PABBIE:
So he's a bit of a fix - er up - per, but this we're cer-tain of:

Ab/Eb
Fm
Fb
Gb
Fb
Gb
fix this fix - er up - per up with a lit - tle bit of love.
With a lit - tle bit of love.
f
Ab
Eb
Gb
Db
Ab
Eb
Gb
Db
E
Cb
Gb
Db
BULDA:
Is it the
WOMEN:
Na na na hei a na. Na na na hei ja nah hi ja na.
MEN:
mf
Ab
Db
HIDDEN FOLK CHILD:
way that he runs scared?
Or that he
HIDDEN FOLK 2:
Or that he's so - cial - ly im - paired?

B♭
E♭
6fr
only likes to tinkle in the woods?
HIDDEN FOLK 3:
Is his
A♭
4fr
D♭
4fr
HIDDEN FOLK 4:
Or the
thick and curly back hair maybe throwing you off track there?
Cm
3fr
Fm9
B♭
E♭
6fr
way he covers up that he's the honest goods?

A♭
G♭/A♭
D♭/A♭
F♭
E♭
WOMEN:
So he's a bit of a fix - er up - per. He's got a coup-le of bugs. His
MEN:
A♭
G♭/A♭
D♭
D♭/C♭
E♭/B♭
E♭
i - so-la - tion is con-fir-ma - tion of his des-per-a - tion for heal-ing hugs.
A♭
G♭/A♭
D♭
A♭/C
B♭7
He's just a bit of a fix - er up - per, but we know what to do. The

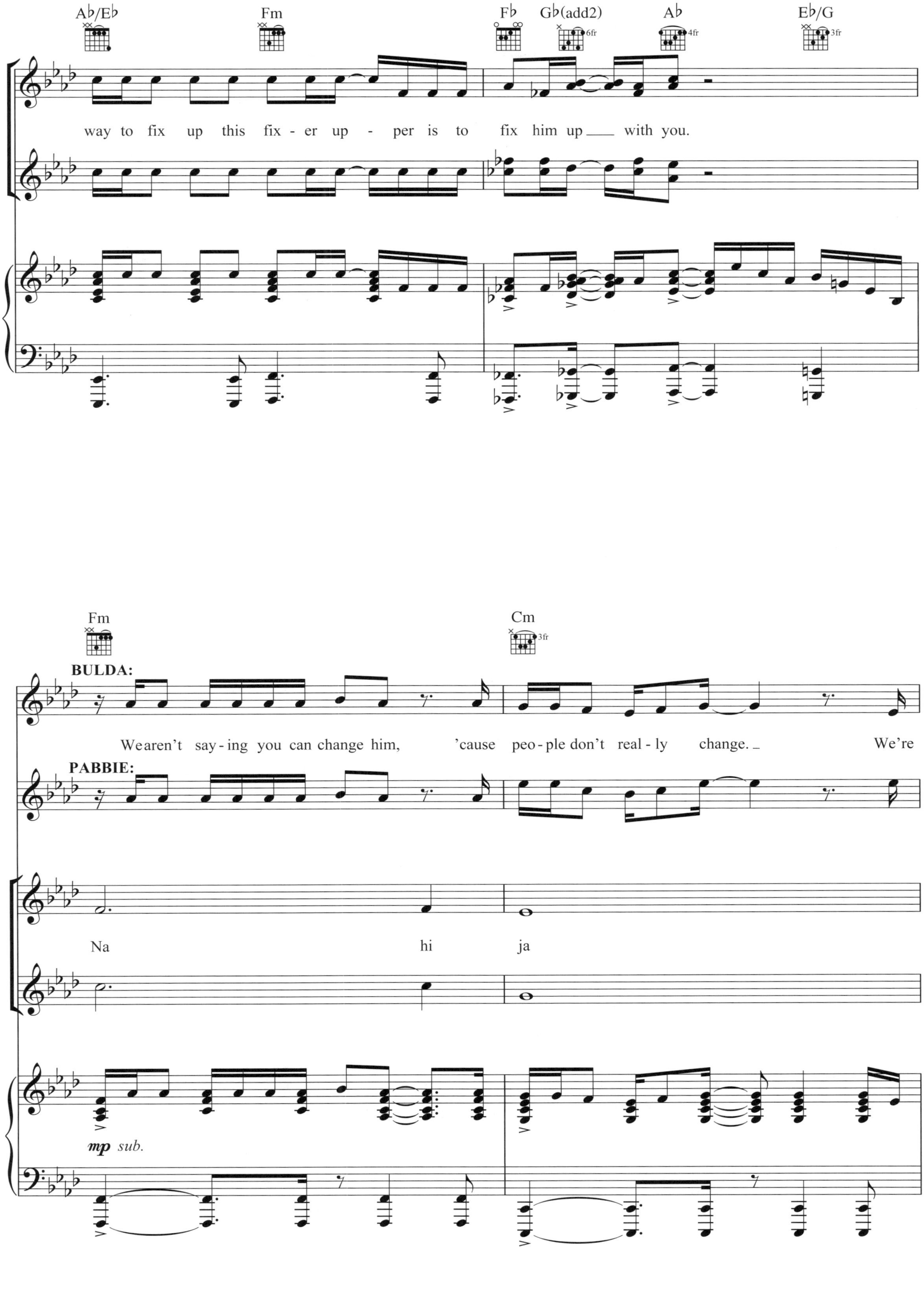

Fm

Cm

3fr

BULDA:

We aren't say - ing you can change him, 'cause peo - ple don't real - ly change. _ We're

PABBIE:

Na hi ja

mp sub.

G♭
D♭
4fr
A♭
4fr
A♭/G♭
4fr
on - ly say - ing that love's a force that's pow - er - ful and strange.
Na
Na hi - ja na.
F
F/A
B♭
Hu-mans make bad choic - es if they're mad or scared or stressed. But
No
No a hei - a no.
mf

C
F/C
C
F/C
C
throw a lit - tle love their way,
and
Throw a lit - tle love their way,
F
B♭/F
F
G♭
C♭/G♭
G♭
you'll bring out their best!
True love brings out the best!
you'll bring out their best!
True love brings out the best!

N.C.
F/A G C Bb/C Bb/E
WOMEN:
Ev-'ry-one's a bit of a fix - er up - per,
MEN:
f
F Ab Bb C Bb/C Bb/E
4fr
that's what it's all a - bout! Fa-ther, sis-ter, broth - er, we need each oth - er to
F G C C/Bb
raise us up and round us out! Ev-'ry one's a bit of a fix - er up - per, but

F6
A♭(add2)
C/G
E+
Am
D7
OLAF:
The only fixer upper fixer that can fix a fixer upper is...
when push comes to shove.
poco accel.
F/D
F/G
C
C/E
WOMEN:
True, true, true, true, true love, true love.
MEN:
True, true, true, true love, true love.
cresc.
f
F
A♭
B♭
C
C/E
F
G
Love, true love, true love. Love, love, true love!
Love, true love, true love. Love, love, true love!
sim.

C
B♭/C
F6
F6/G
A♭
4fr
Ev-'ry-one's a bit of a fix - er up - per but ver - y wor - thy of
C/G
Am
B♭
C
F
love! True love!
ff
C
Fm7
Gm7
C
True love!
sfz

KRISTOFF LULLABY

Music and Lyrics by KRISTEN ANDERSON-LOPEZ
and ROBERT LOPEZ

A9/C♯
D
D/C
G/B
C
you.
You light the world for me.
You live life fear-less-ly,
Em
Bm/D
C
F/C
C
D
D/C
brav-er than the brav-est of us do.
You trust, you hope, you dare,
G/B
C
Am7
G
you choose to feel and care.
I thought that I was strong 'til
colla voce
F
C
D
E♭
B♭
6fr
I bumped in-to you.
What do I know a-bout
a tempo
mf

G
G/F♯
E♭
B♭/D
Gm
F
G
G/F♯
love?
What do I know a - bout love?
E♭
B♭maj7/D
B♭m/D♭
Csus
C
Ev - 'ry - thing I thought I did,
you've gone and changed it, kid.
poco rit.
mp
E♭
B♭/D
Fsus
You're what I know a - bout
a tempo
rit.
G
G/F♯
E♭
B♭/D
B♭
F6/A
G
love.
a tempo

MONSTER

Music and Lyrics by KRISTEN ANDERSON-LOPEZ
and ROBERT LOPEZ

C
Dm
B♭
time's run-ning out. Don't feel, don't feel. Fear will be your en-e-my and
Fsus
F
C
Csus
3fr
death its con-se-quence. That's what they once said to me, and it's
Dm
F/C
B♭
F
start-ing to make sense. All this pain, all this fear be-gan be-cause of me.
E♭
6fr
Asus
A
Asus2
A5
5fr
Is the thing they see the thing I have to be? A

Bm
F♯m/A
E/G♯
G5
3fr
mon - ster. Were they right? Has the dark in me fi - n'lly come to light? Am I a
mp
Bm
F♯m
E/G♯
mon - ster, full of rage, no - where to go but on a
G5
3fr
B♭
Gm7
ram - page? Or, am I just a mon - ster in a
Faster, driving
D5
5fr
Dm/F
Gsus2
B♭sus2
HANS:
cage? No harm comes to her.
MEN:
End this win - ter. Bring back sum - mer. Keep your guard up!
f

D5
5fr
Dm/F
Gsus2
B♭sus2
MEN:
End this win-ter. Bring back sum-mer. Keep your guard up!
Dm
B♭/D
A7/C♯
ELSA:
What do I do? No time for cry-ing now. I start-ed a storm, got-ta
mf
Dm
B♭
F
stop it some-how. Do I keep on run-ning? How far do I have to go? And
Csus
3fr
C
Dm
F/C
B♭
would that take the storm a-way or on-ly make it grow? I'm mak-ing my world cold-er. How

Fsus F E♭ A7sus
long can it sur-vive? Is ev-'ry-one in dan-ger as long as I'm a-live?
A Bm F♯m/A E/G♯
Was I a mon-ster from the start? How did I end up with this fro-zen
G Bm F♯m E/G♯
heart, bring-ing de-struc-tion to the stage, caught in a war that I nev-er meant to
Faster still
Gsus2 D/G B♭ Gm7
wage? Do I kill the mon-ster?

Freely
Bm
F♯m/A
E/G♯
Fa - ther, you know what's best for me.
If I die, will
mp
G
Bm
F♯m/A
E/G♯
they be free?
Moth - er, what if af - ter I'm gone the cold gets cold - er and the
In tempo
G
Bm
storm rag - es on?
No!
I have to stay a - live to
F♯m/A
E
fix what I've done.
Save the world from my - self and

Gsus2
G(add2)
G5
3fr
bring back the sun.
If I'm a
VOLUNTEERS:
Ah.
cresc.
poco accel.
Cm
3fr
Gm/B♭
F/A
mon - ster and it's true, there's on - ly one thing that's left for me to
End this win - ter. Bring back sum - mer. Keep your guard
ff
A♭
4fr
Cm
3fr
Gm
3fr
do. But be - fore I fade to white, I'll do
up! End this win - ter. Bring back sum - mer.

F/A
A♭sus2
E♭/A♭
A♭m6/C♭
all that I can to make things right. I can-not be a mon - ster.
Keep your guard up!
mf
A♭m7
I will not be a mon - ster. Not to-night!
E♭m
E♭m/D♭
E♭m/C
E♭m/A
E♭5
Mon - ster!
ENSEMBLE:
Mon - ster! Mon - ster!
f

TRUE LOVE

Music and Lyrics by KRISTEN ANDERSON-LOPEZ
and ROBERT LOPEZ

Dm
sto - ries told of true love.
How I'd find
mp
E♭maj9
6fr
B♭5
true love.
And here I am in this
F/B♭
E♭5/B♭
6fr
F/B♭
B♭5
room a - gain,
just as lost and small.
That
E♭/B♭
6fr
B♭sus
A♭
4fr
lone - ly girl with a des - p'rate heart is who I am,

F
B♭
F/B♭
af - ter all.
There's no es - cap - ing her,
but now the dream is gone
E♭/B♭
6fr
E♭m/B♭
6fr
Dm
3
be - cause I spent a life - time count - ing on
true
love,
E♭maj9
6fr
3
true
love.
cresc.
Gm
3fr
C
Gm
3fr
I was look - ing for a fair - y tale and dove head - first in - to
f

C
E♭
6fr
his.
Turns out, you can't find love if you don't know what it
mf
Fsus
F
B♭5
is.
And now it's clear I'll nev - er
mp
F/B♭
E♭(add2)/B♭
6fr
F/B♭
leave this room. It ends as it be - gan,
E♭
6fr
B♭sus
A♭(add2)
4fr
with no one but my - self to blame. I played my part

Freely
F
B♭5
F/B♭
in the plan. Dream-ing got me here, and yet the dream won't die. I
E♭(add2)/B♭
E♭m/B♭
Dm
can't wish it a-way, no mat-ter how I try. True love,
mf a tempo
E♭maj9
B♭(add2)
true love, true love.
B♭(add2)/A♭
E♭
B♭
poco rit.

COLDER BY THE MINUTE

Music and Lyrics by KRISTEN ANDERSON-LOPEZ
and ROBERT LOPEZ

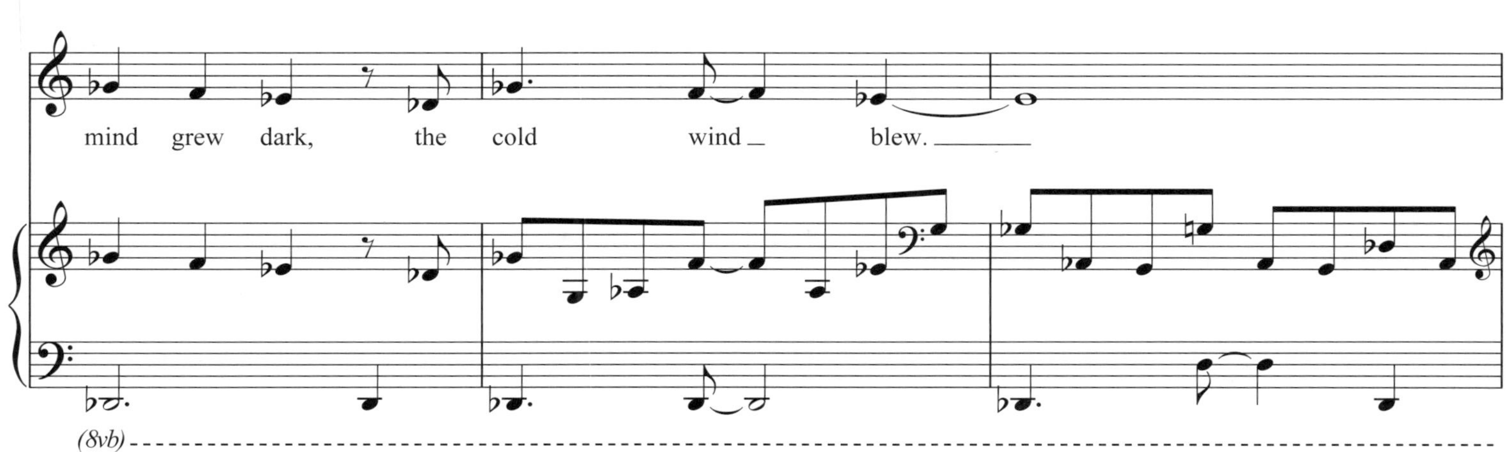

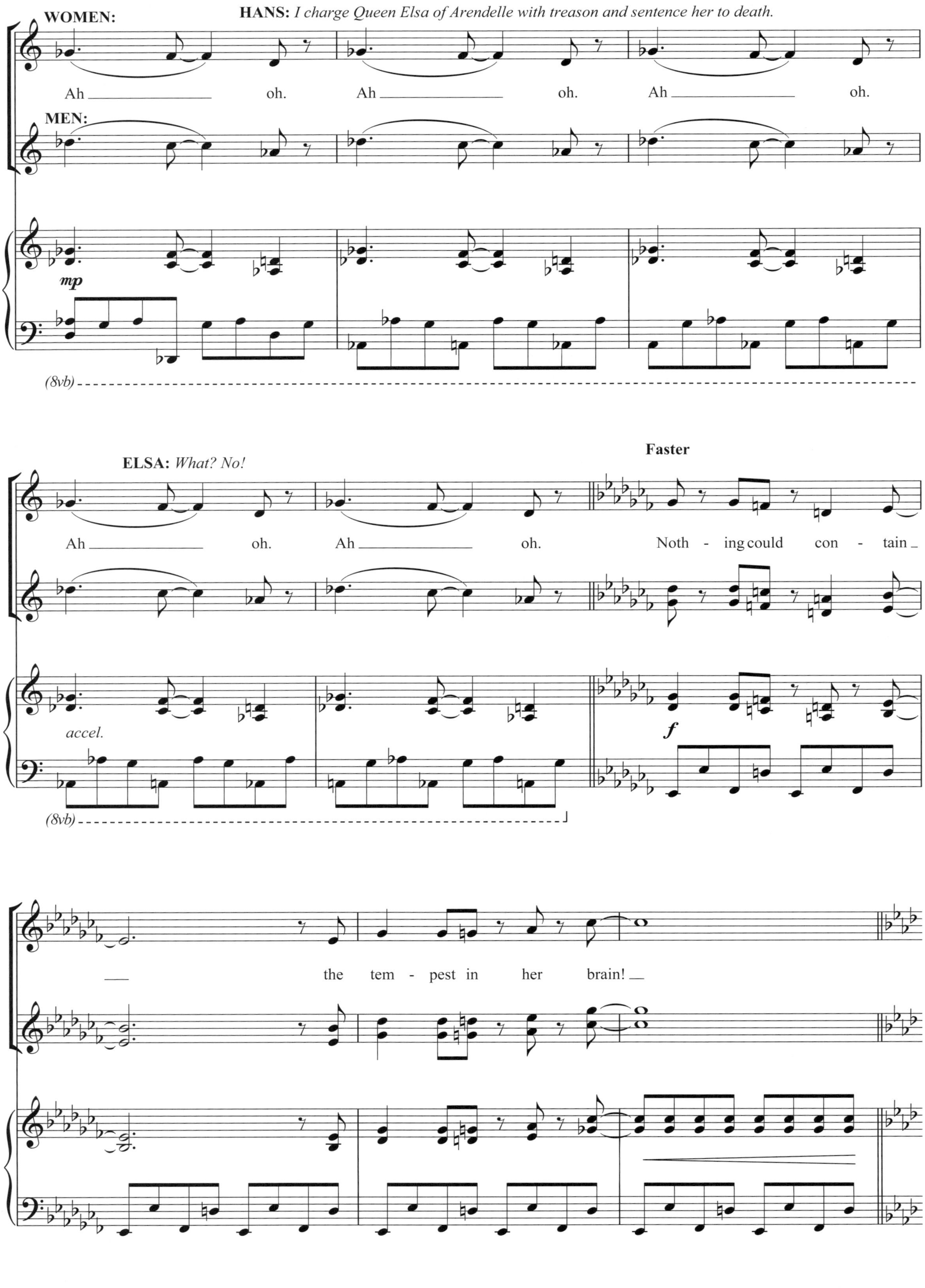

WOMEN:
HANS: I charge Queen Elsa of Arendelle with treason and sentence her to death.
Ah oh. Ah oh. Ah oh.
MEN:
mp
(8vb)
ELSA: What? No!
Faster
Ah oh. Ah oh. Noth - ing could con - tain
accel.
f
(8vb)
the tem - pest in her brain!

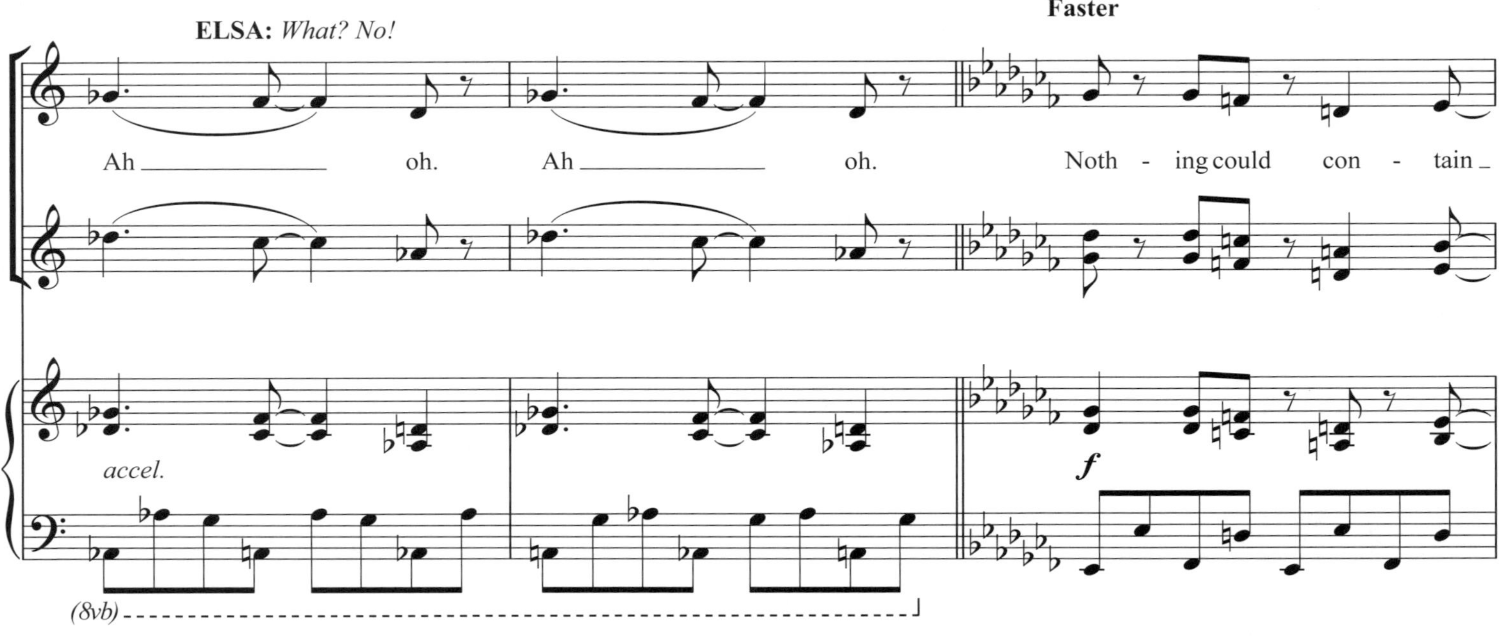

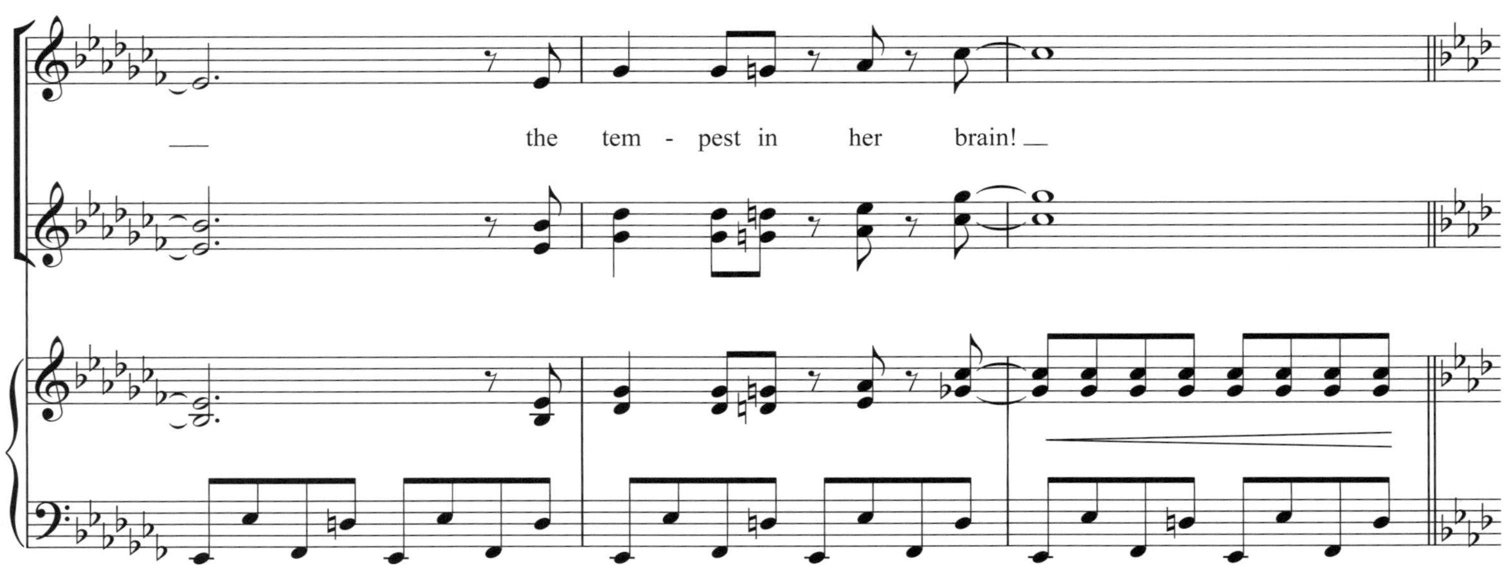

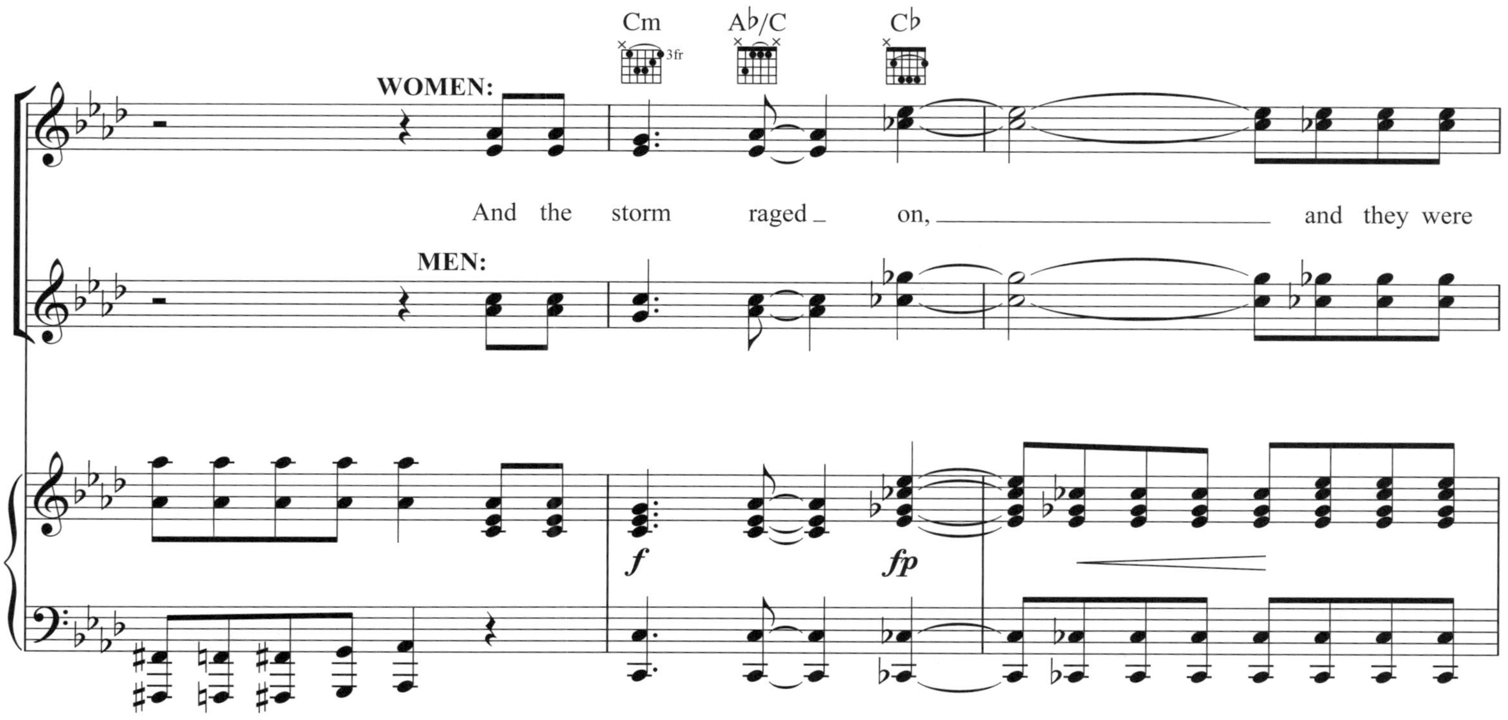
Cm
A♭/C
C♭
3fr
WOMEN:
And the storm raged _ on, ___ and they were
MEN:
f
fp

D♭5
A♭m7
A♭
Cm
A♭/C
C♭
4fr
3fr
rav - aged by ___ the wrath ___ of snow. _ And the wind blew _ fear, ___
fp

D♭
B♭sus
and the storm would grow
E♭5
E♭5/E
E♭5
E♭5/E
WOMEN & MEN:
cold - er by the min - ute, cold - er by the min - ute.
mf
Cm
E
Cm
ANNA:
Keep walk - ing, An - na, don't stop, don't rest. He's out here some - where.

Gm
Ab
Eb/Ab
I can feel the ice in my chest,
Db/Ab
G7
Cm
in my heart, I don't care. I've got to reach you through the
E
Cm
Gm
storm some - how, be - cause the one thing that can save me now is your
Ab
Bb/Ab
love. True love!
KRISTOFF:
An - na! Where are
f
cresc.

Eb5
6fr
Eb5/E
Eb5
6fr
Eb5/E
Eb5
6fr
you?
WOMEN & MEN:
Cold - er by the min - ute, cold - er by the min - ute.
mf
Ab
4fr
Abm
4fr
Ab
4fr
Abm
4fr
ELSA:
Can't run, can't stop, can't breathe, can't live and I can't die.
HANS:
El - sa, lis - ten!
MEN:
Hah
mf

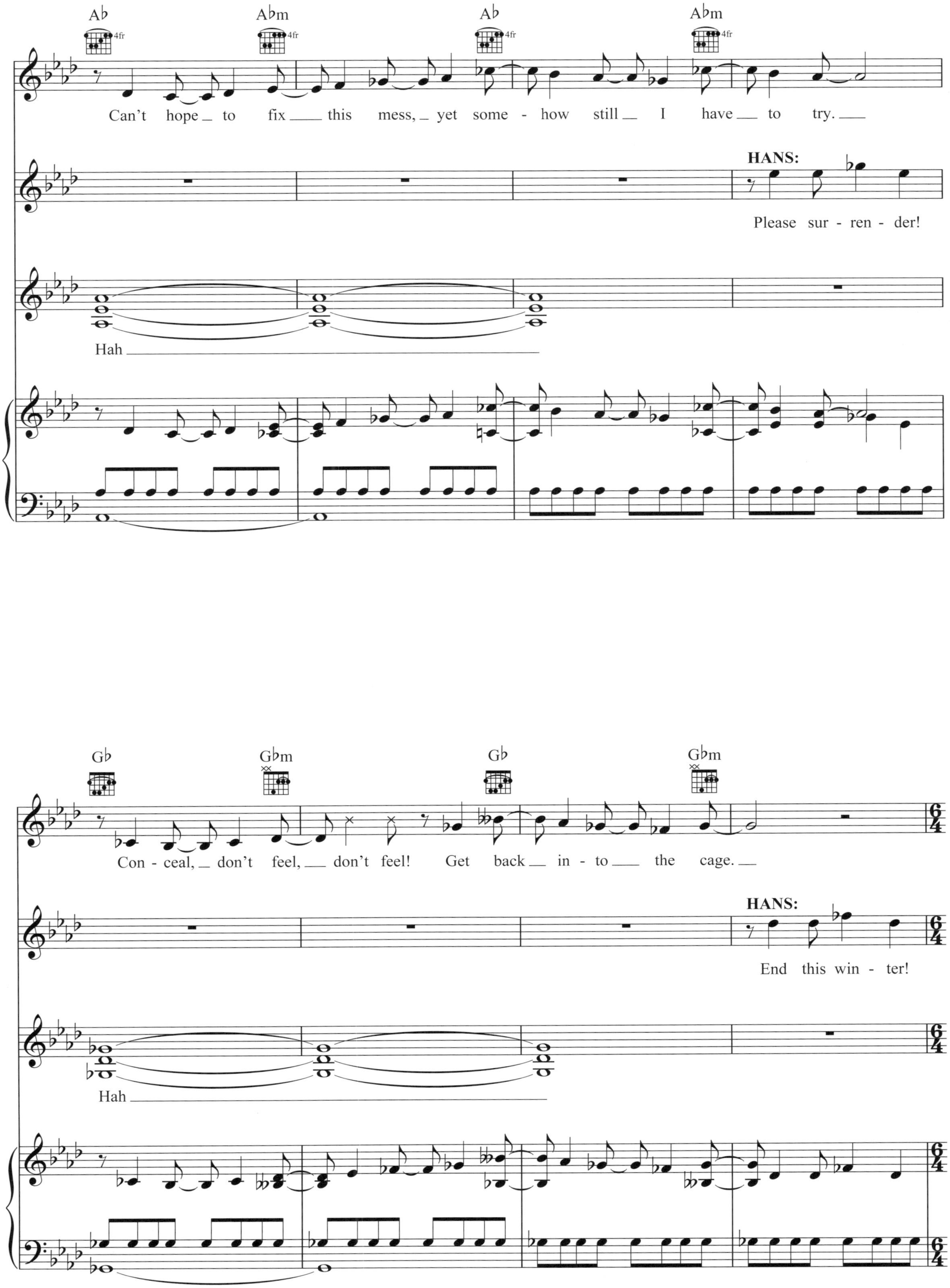

A♭ 4fr
A♭m 4fr
A♭ 4fr
A♭m 4fr

Can't hope _ to fix ___ this mess, _ yet some - how still _ I have ___ to try. ___

HANS:

Please sur - ren - der!

Hah ___

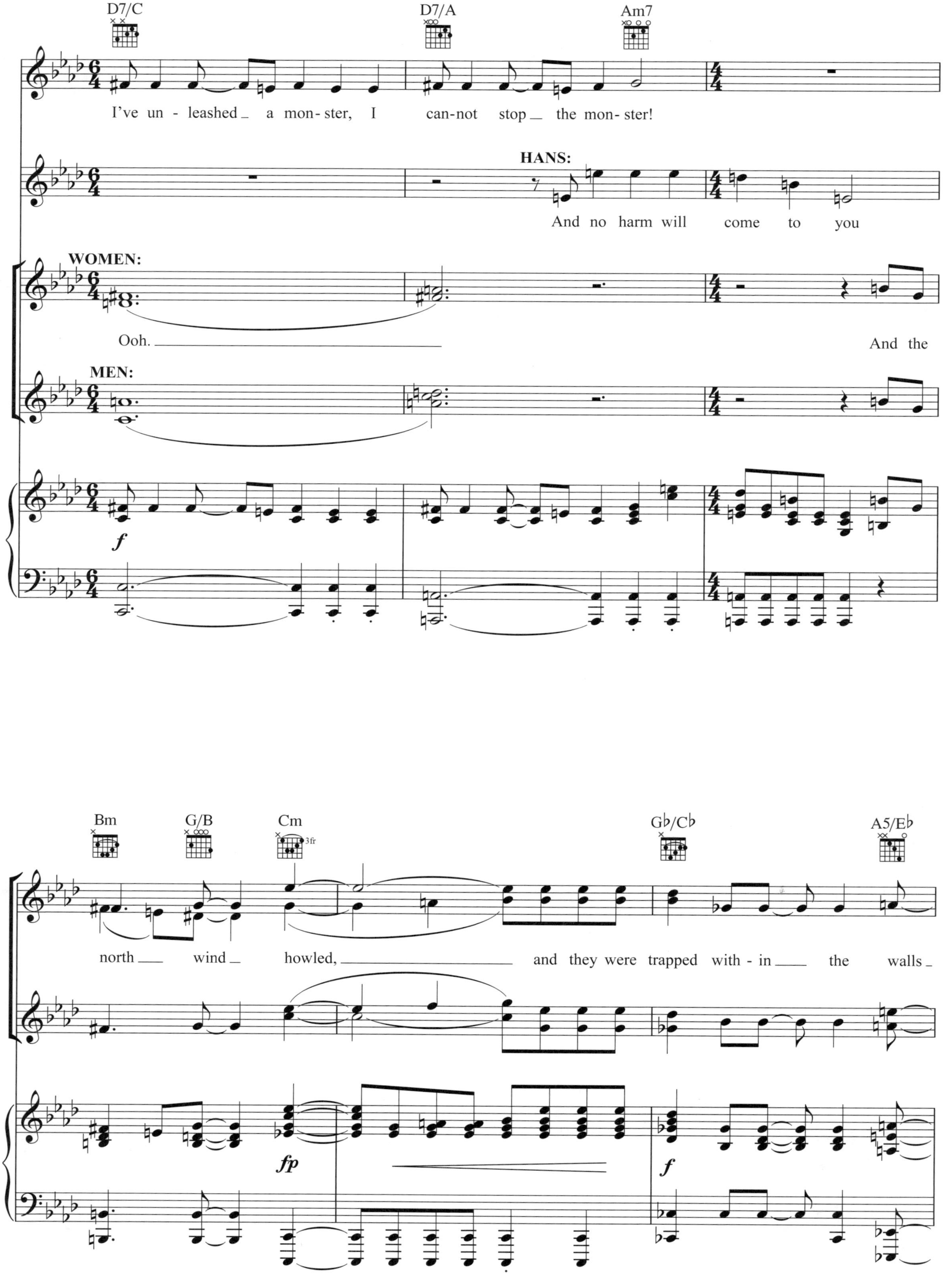

D7/C D7/A Am7

I've un - leashed a mon - ster, I can - not stop the mon - ster!

HANS:

And no harm will come to you

WOMEN:

Ooh. And the

MEN:

f

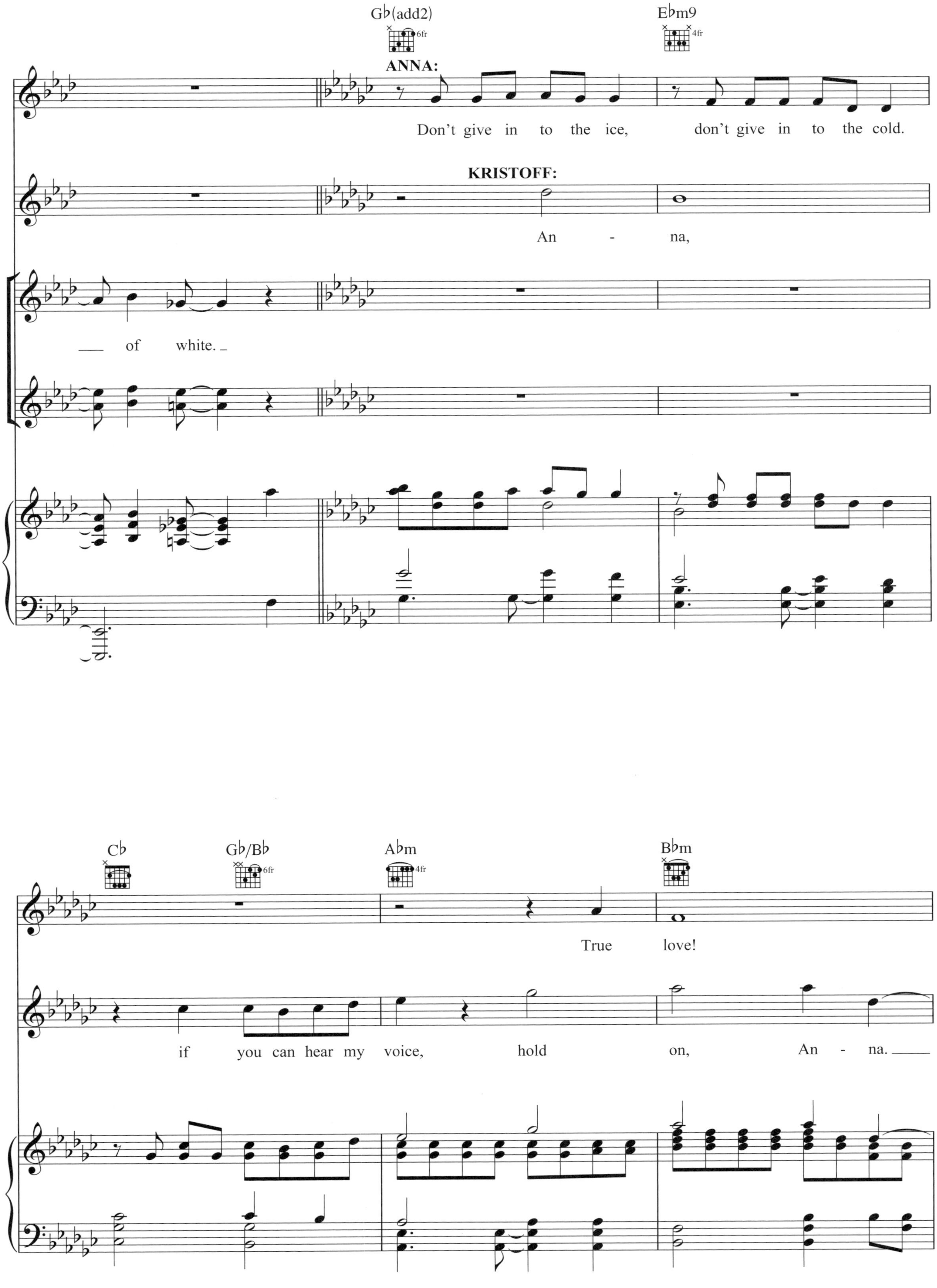

G♭(add2) 6fr
E♭m9 4fr

ANNA:
Don't give in to the ice, don't give in to the cold.

KRISTOFF:
An - na,

___ of white. _

E♭m

ELSA:

I can't!

HANS:

El - sa!

WOMEN:

And the

MEN:

cresc.

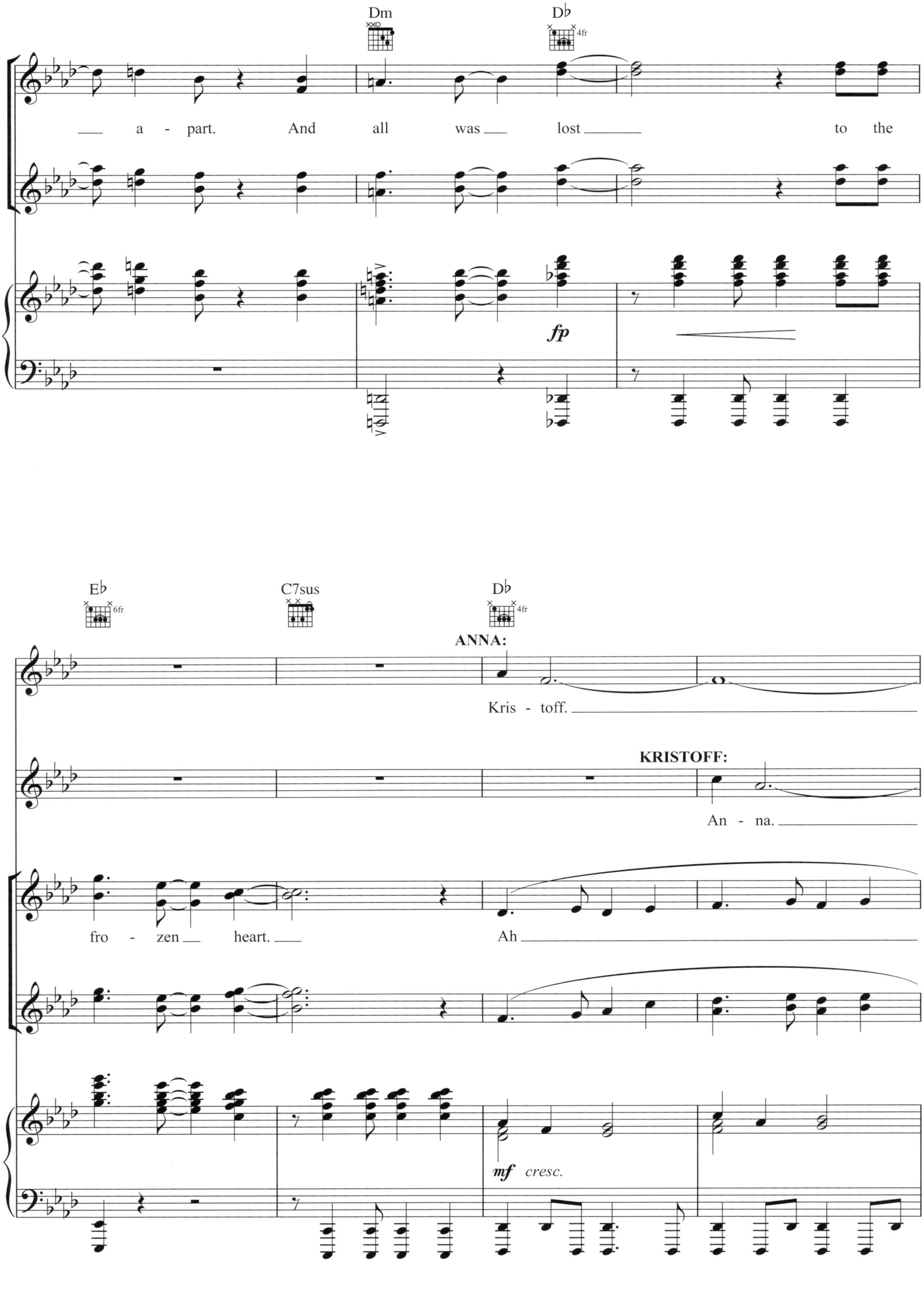

E♭ 6fr C7sus D♭ 4fr

ANNA:

Kris - toff.

KRISTOFF:

An - na.

fro - zen heart. Ah

mf cresc.

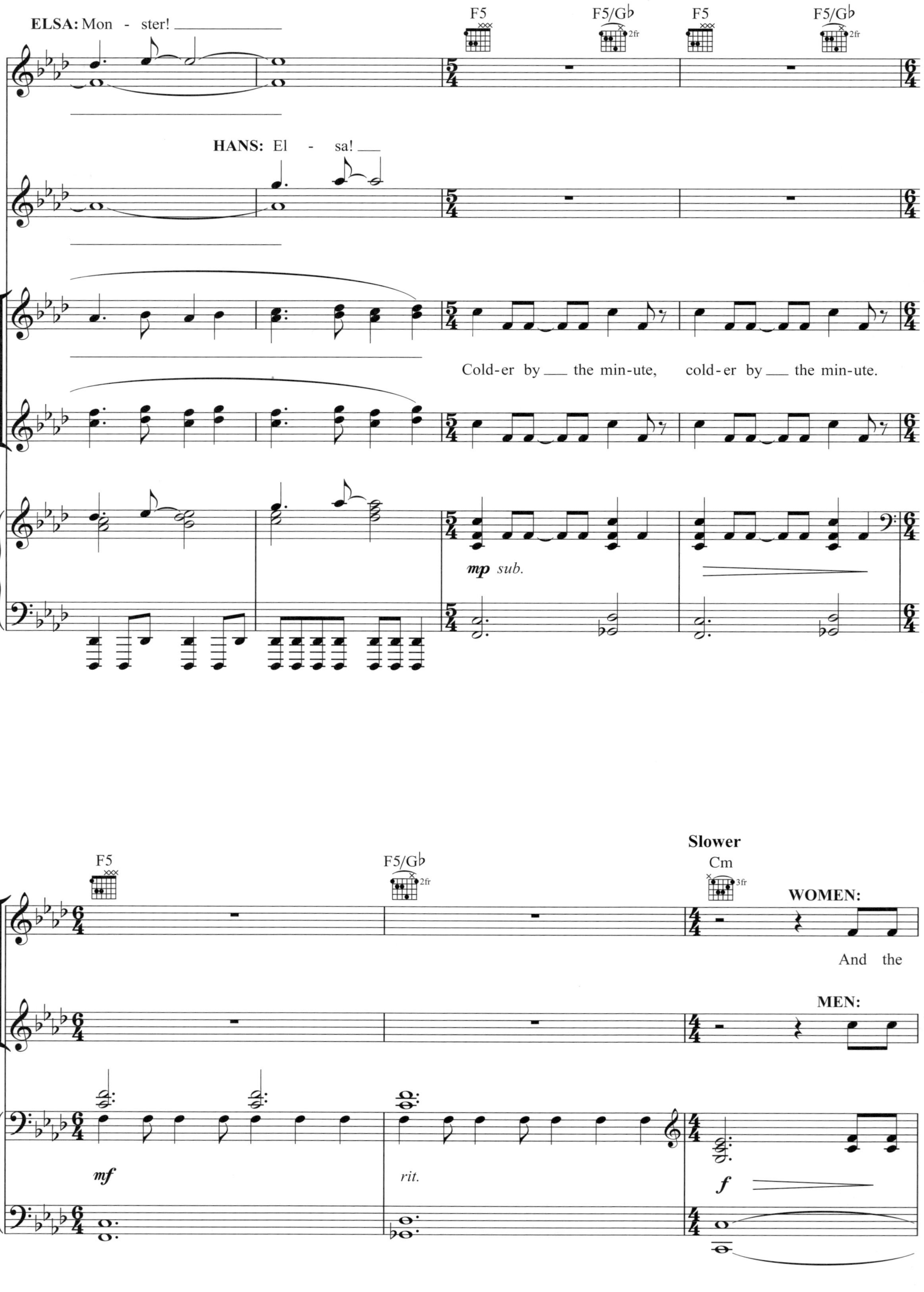

F5 F5/G♭ F5 F5/G♭

ELSA: Mon - ster!

HANS: El - sa!

Cold-er by the min-ute, cold-er by the min-ute.

mp sub.

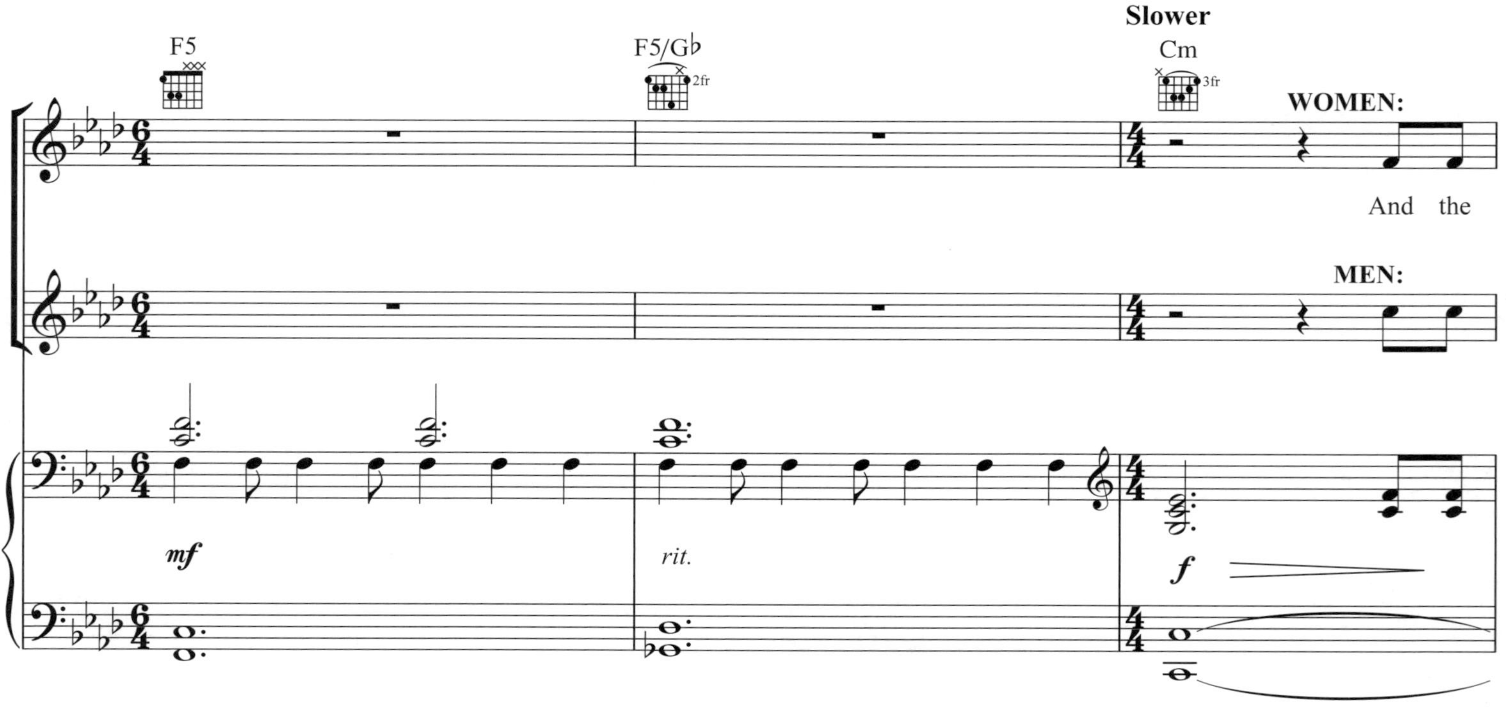

N.C.
wind blew soft, and in her grief, the storm stood still.
mp
F/A
Am
B♭
Cm
3fr
mf
Moderately fast
Dm
C
F5/C
B♭
F/A
Gm7
f
B♭m
Cm
WOMEN:
Ah
MEN:
f
cresc.
rit.